D0985603

Table of Contents

Timeless Grace Tank, *page 33*

Corded Shells Cowl Top *page 9*

Eyelet Dream Tank *page 25*

Anytime Tee

Skill Level

■■■□ INTERMEDIATE

Finished Sizes

Instructions given fit size small; changes for medium, large, X-large, 2X-large, 3X-large and 4X-large are in [ ].

Finished Measurement

Bust: 36 inches *(small)* [40 inches *(medium)*, 44 inches *(large)*, 48 inches *(X-large)*, 52 inches *(2X-large)*, 56 inches *(3X-large)*, 60 inches *(4X-large)*]

Materials

- Omega Dalia size 3 crochet cotton (3½ oz/404 yds/100g per ball): 4 [4, 5, 6, 6, 7, 7] balls #509 phosphorus
- Size G/6/4mm crochet hook or size needed to obtain gauge
- Tapestry needle

Gauge

24 sts = 4 inches; 12 pattern rows = 4 inches

Pattern Notes

Weave in ends as work progresses.

Chain-3 at beginning of row counts as first double crochet unless otherwise stated.

Chain-2 at beginning of row counts as first half double crochet unless otherwise stated.

Join with slip stitch as indicated unless otherwise stated.

Chain-3 at beginning of round counts as first double crochet unless otherwise stated.

On row 1 of Front, each chain-3 counts as a double crochet.

Special Stitch

Single crochet shell (sc shell): (Sc, ch 2, sc) in st indicated.

Tee

Body

Row 1 (WS): Ch 68, **sc shell** *(see Special Stitch)* in 3rd ch from hook (beg 2 sk chs count as a hdc), *sk next 2 chs, sc shell in next ch, rep from * across to last 2 chs, sk next ch, hdc in last ch, turn. *(22 sc shells, 2 hdc)*

Row 2 (RS): Ch 3 *(see Pattern Notes)*, sk first 2 sts, *3 dc in next ch-2 sp**, sk next 2 sc, rep from * across, ending last rep at **, dc in 2nd ch of beg 2 sk chs, turn. *(68 dc)*

Row 3: Ch 2 *(see Pattern Notes)*, sk first 2 sts, *sc shell in next dc**, sk next 2 dc, rep from * across, ending last rep at **, sk next dc, hdc in last dc, turn.

Row 4: Ch 3, sk first 2 sts, *3 dc in next ch-2 sp**, sk next 2 sc, rep from * across, ending last rep at **, dc in last hdc, turn. *(68 dc)*

Rows 5–108 [5–120, 5–132, 5–144, 5–156, 5–168, 5–180]: [Rep rows 3 and 4 alternately] 52 [58, 64, 70, 76, 82, 88] times.

Row 109 [121, 133, 145, 157, 169, 181]: With RS tog, bring foundation ch behind work, ch 1, sl st in first foundation ch, sk first 2 dc on working row, *sl st in next dc, sk next foundation ch, sl st in next ch-2 sp of foundation**, sk next 2 dc on working row, rep from * across, ending last rep at **, sl st in last dc of working row, ch 1, turn to work in ends of rows.

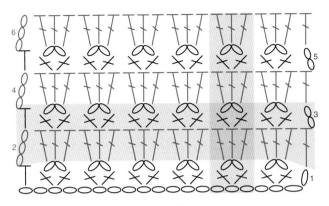

Anytime Tee
Reduced Sample of Stitch Diagram
Note: *Reps shown in gray.*

<table>
<tr><td colspan="2">STITCH KEY</td></tr>
<tr><td>◯</td><td>Chain (ch)</td></tr>
<tr><td>+</td><td>Single crochet (sc)</td></tr>
<tr><td>T</td><td>Half double crochet (hdc)</td></tr>
<tr><td>Ŧ</td><td>Double crochet (dc)</td></tr>
<tr><td>⤙⤚
╳ ╳</td><td>Single crochet shell
(sc shell)</td></tr>
</table>

Bottom Edging

Rnd 1: Working on WS in ends of rows, sc shell in first row, *sk next row, [sc shell in next row] twice, rep from * around to last 2 rows, sk next row, sc shell in last row, **join** *(see Pattern Notes)* in first sc. Fasten off. *(72 [80, 88, 96, 104, 112, 120] sc shells)*

Bodice

Rnd 1: With WS facing, working in ends of rows on opposite side of Body, join yarn in last row, ch 1, sc shell in first row, *sk next row, [sc shell in next row] twice, rep from * around to last 2 rows, sk next row, sc shell in last row, join in first sc, sl st in next ch-2 sp, turn. *(72 [80, 88, 96, 104, 112, 120] sc shells)*

Rnd 2: Ch 3 *(see Pattern Notes)*, dc in same ch-2 sp, *sk next 2 sc**, 3 dc in next ch-2 sp, rep from * around, ending last rep at **, dc in same ch-2 sp as beg ch-3, join in 3rd ch of beg ch-3, turn. *(216 [240, 264, 288, 312, 336, 360] dc)*

Sizes Small, Medium, Large & X-Large Only

Rnd 3: Ch 1, sc in first dc, *sk next 2 dc**, sc shell in next dc, rep from * around, ending last rep at **, sc in same dc as first sc, ch 2, join in first sc. Fasten off.

Sizes 2X-Large & 3X-Large Only

Rnd [3]: Ch 1, sc in first dc, *sk next 2 dc**, sc shell in next dc, rep from * around, ending last rep at **, sc in same dc as first sc, ch 2, join in first sc, sl st in next ch-2 sp, turn.

Rnd [4]: Ch 3, dc in same ch-2 sp, *sk next 2 sc**, 3 dc in next ch-2 sp, rep from * around, ending last rep at **, dc in same ch-2 sp as beg ch-3, join in 3rd ch of beg ch-3, turn.

Rnd [5]: Ch 1, sc in first dc, *sk next 2 dc**, sc shell in next dc, rep from * around, ending last rep at **, sc in same dc as first sc, ch 2, join in first sc. Fasten off.

Size 4X-Large Only

Rnd [3]: Ch 1, sc in first dc, *sk next 2 dc**, sc shell in next dc, rep from * around, ending last rep at **, sc in same dc as first sc, ch 2, join in first sc, sl st in next ch-2 sp, turn.

Rnd [4]: Ch 3, dc in same ch-2 sp, *sk next 2 sc**, 3 dc in next ch-2 sp, rep from * around, ending last rep at **, dc in same ch-2 sp as beg ch-3, join in 3rd ch of beg ch-3, turn.

Rnd [5]: Ch 1, sc in first dc, *sk next 2 dc**, sc shell in next dc, rep from * around, ending last rep at **, sc in same dc as first sc, ch 2, join in first sc, sl st in next ch-2 sp, turn.

Rnd [6]: Rep rnd 4.

Rnd [7]: Ch 1, sc in first dc, *sk next 2 dc**, sc shell in next dc, rep from * around, ending last rep at **, sc in same dc as first sc, ch 2, join in first sc. Fasten off.

Back

Row 1: Ch 31, with RS of Bodice facing, 3 dc in last ch-2 sp made on Bodice, [sk next 2 sc, 3 dc in next ch-2 sp] 35 [39, 43, 47, 51, 55, 59] times, ch 31, turn. *(108 [120, 132, 144, 156, 168, 180] dc)*

Row 2: Sc shell in 3rd ch from hook (beg 2 sk chs count as a hdc), *[sk next 2 chs, sc shell in next ch] 9 times, sk next ch*, sk next dc, [sc shell in next dc, sk next 2 dc] 35 [39, 43, 47, 51, 55, 59] times, sc shell in next dc, sk next dc and next ch, sc shell in next ch, rep from * to *, hdc in last ch, turn. *(56 [60, 64, 68, 72, 76, 80] sc shells)*

Row 3: Ch 3, sk first 2 sts, *3 dc in next ch-2 sp**, sk next 2 sc, rep from * to last 8 ch-2 sps, ending last rep at **, sc in next ch-2 sp, leaving rem sts unworked, turn. *(145 [157, 169, 181, 193, 205, 217] dc, 1 sc)*

Row 4: Ch 1, sk first 2 sts, [sc shell in next dc, sk next 2 dc] 41 [45, 49, 53, 57, 61, 65] times, sc in next dc, turn. *(41 [45, 49, 53, 57, 61, 65] sc shells, 1 sc)*

Row 5: Ch 1, sk first 2 sts, *3 dc in next ch-2 sp**, sk next 2 sc, rep from * across, ending last rep at **, sk next sc, 3 dc in sc 2 rows below, sk next 2 sc 3 rows below, sc in next ch-2 sp, turn. *(126 [138, 150, 162, 174, 186, 198] dc, 1 sc)*

Row 6: Ch 1, sk first 2 sts, *sc shell in next dc**, sk next 2 dc, rep from * across, ending last rep at **, sk next dc and next ch-1 sp, sc shell in sc 2 rows below, sk next 2 dc 3 rows below, sc in next dc, ch 1, turn. *(43 [47, 51, 55, 59, 63, 67] sc shells, 1 sc)*

Row 7: Ch 1, sk first 2 sts, *3 dc in next ch-2 sp**, sk next 2 sc, rep from * across, ending last rep at **, sk next sc, 3 dc in sc 2 rows below, sk next 2 sc on row 2 below, sc in next ch-2 sp, turn. *(132 [144, 156, 168, 180, 192, 204] dc, 1 sc)*

Row 8: Ch 1, sk first 2 sts, *sc shell in next dc**, sk next 2 dc, rep from * across, ending last rep at **, sk next dc and next ch-1 sp, sc shell in sc 2 rows below, sk next 2 dc on row 3 below, sc in next dc, ch 1, turn. *(45 [49, 53, 57, 61, 65, 69] sc shells, 1 sc)*

Row 9: Ch 1, sk first 2 sts, *3 dc in next ch-2 sp**, sk next 2 sc, rep from * across, ending last rep at **, sk next sc, 3 dc in sc 2 rows below, sk next 2 sc on row 2 below, sc in next ch-2 sp, turn. *(138 [150, 162, 174, 186, 198, 210] dc, 1 sc)*

Row 10: Ch 1, sk first 2 sts, *sc shell in next dc**, sk next 2 dc, rep from * across, ending last rep at **, sk next dc and next ch-1 sp, sc shell in sc 2 rows below, sk next 2 dc on row 3 below, sc in next dc, ch 1, turn. *(47 [51, 55, 59, 63, 67, 71] sc shells, 1 sc)*

Row 11: Ch 1, sk first 2 sts, *3 dc in next ch-2 sp**, sk next 2 sc, rep from * across, ending last rep at **, sk next sc and next ch-1 sp, 3 dc in sc 2 rows below, [sk next 2 sc on row 2 below, 3 dc in next ch-2 sp] 4 times, sk next sc, dc in last sc, turn. *(157 [169, 181, 193, 205, 217, 229] dc)*

Row 12: Ch 2, sk first 2 sts, *sc shell in next dc**, sk next 2 dc, rep from * across, ending last rep at **, sk next dc, sc shell in sc 2 rows below, [sk next 2 dc on row 3 below, sc shell in next dc] 3 times, sk next dc, hdc in last dc, turn. *(56 [60, 64, 68, 72, 76, 80] sc shells, 2 hdc)*

Row 13: Ch 3, sk first 2 sts, *3 dc in next ch-2 sp**, sk next 2 sc, rep from * across, ending last rep at **, dc in last hdc, turn. *(170 [182, 194, 206, 218, 230, 242] dc)*

Row 14: Ch 2, sk first 2 sts, *sc shell in next dc**, sk next 2 dc, rep from * across, ending last rep at **, sk next dc, hdc in last dc, turn.

Rows 15–26 [15–28, 15–30, 15–32, 15–32, 15–34, 15–36]: [Rep rows 13 and 14 alternately] 6 [7, 8, 9, 9, 10, 11] times.

Row 27 [29, 31, 33, 33, 35, 37]: Rep row 13.

Left Shoulder

Row 1: Ch 2, sk first 2 sts, [sc shell in next dc, sk next 2 dc] 23 [25, 27, 28, 30, 32, 34] times, hdc in next dc, leaving rem sts unworked, turn. *(23 [25, 27, 28, 30, 32, 34] shells, 2 hdc)*

Row 2: Ch 3, sk first 2 sts, dc in next ch-2 sp, *sk next 2 sc, 3 dc in next ch-2 sp, rep from * across, sk next sc, dc in last hdc. Fasten off. *(69 [75, 81, 84, 90, 96, 102] dc)*

Right Shoulder

Row 1: With WS facing, sk next 26 [26, 26, 32, 32, 32, 32] dc from Left Shoulder, join yarn in next dc, ch 2, *sk next 2 dc, sc shell in next dc, rep from * across, sk next dc, dc in last hdc, turn. *(23 [25, 27, 28, 30, 32, 34] shells, 2 hdc)*

Row 2: Ch 3, sk first 2 sts, *3 dc in next ch-2 sp, sk next 2 sc, rep from * until 1 ch-2 sp rem, dc in next ch-2 sp, dc in last hdc. Fasten off. *(69 [75, 81, 84, 90, 96, 102] dc)*

Front

Row 1: With RS facing and working in foundation chs of sleeves and front of Body, join yarn in first ch of right sleeve, ch 3, [sk next 2 ch, 3 dc in next ch] 9 times, sk next 2 ch, (2 dc, **ch 3** *(see Pattern Notes)*, sl st) in next ch, (sl st, ch 3, 2 dc) in next ch-2 sp, [sk next 2 sc, 3 dc in next ch-2 sp] 34 [38, 40, 44, 48, 52, 56] times, sk next 2 sc, (2 dc, ch 3, sl st) in next ch-2 sp, sk next 2 ch, (sl st, ch 3, 2 dc) in next ch, [sk next 2 ch, 3 dc in next ch] 9 times, sk next ch, dc in last ch, turn. *(170 [182, 194, 206, 218, 230, 242] dc)*

Row 2: Ch 2, sk first 2 sts, *sc shell in next dc**, sk next 2 dc, rep from * across, ending last rep at **, sk next dc, hdc in last dc, turn. *(56 [60, 64, 68, 72, 76, 80] sc shells)*

Rows 3–12: Rep rows 3–12 of Back.

Row 13: Ch 3, sk first 2 sts, *3 dc in next ch-2 sp**, sk next 2 sc, rep from * across, ending last rep at **, dc in last hdc, turn. *(170 [182, 194, 206, 218, 230, 242] dc)*

Row 14: Ch 2, sk first 2 sts, *sc shell in next dc**, sk next 2 dc, rep from * across, ending last rep at **, sk next dc, hdc in last dc, turn.

Rows 15–18 [15–20, 15–22, 15–24, 15–24, 15–26, 15–28]: [Rep rows 13 and 14 alternately] 2 [3, 4, 5, 5, 6, 7] times.

Row 19 [21, 23, 25, 25, 27, 29]: Rep row 13.

Neck/Right Shoulder Shaping

Row 1 (RS): Ch 2, sk first 2 sts, [sc shell in next dc, sk next 2 dc] 25 [27, 29, 30, 32, 34, 36] times, hdc in next dc, leaving rem sts unworked, turn. *(25 [27, 29, 30, 32, 34, 36] shells, 2 hdc)*

Row 2: Ch 3, sk first 2 sts, dc in next ch-2 sp, *sk next 2 sc, 3 dc in next ch-2 sp, rep from * across, sk next dc, dc in last hdc, turn. *(75 [81, 87, 90, 96, 102, 108] dc)*

Row 3: Ch 2, sk first 2 sts, [sc shell in next dc, sk next 2 dc] 23 [25, 27, 28, 30, 32, 34] times, hdc in next dc, turn. *(23 [25, 27, 28, 30, 32, 34] shells, 2 hdc)*

Row 4: Rep row 2. *(69 [75, 81, 87, 90, 96, 102] dc)*

Row 5: Ch 2, sk first 2 sts, *sc shell in next dc, sk next 2 dc, rep from * across, hdc in last dc, turn. *(22 [24, 26, 27, 29, 31, 33] sc shells, 2 hdc)*

Row 6: Ch 3, sk first 2 sts, *3 dc in next ch-2 sp**, sk next 2 sc, rep from * across, ending last rep at **, dc in last hdc, turn. *(68 [74, 80, 86, 89, 95, 101] dc)*

Row 7: Ch 2, sk first 2 sts, *sc shell in next dc**, sk next 2 dc, rep from * across, ending last rep at **, sk next dc, hdc in last dc, turn.

Row 8: Rep row 6.

Row 9: Hold Front and Back Shoulders with RS tog, ch 1, sl st in first dc of back, ch 1, *sk 2 dc on front**, sc in next dc, sk next dc on Back Shoulder, [sl st in next dc] twice, sc in same dc on front, rep from * across, ending last rep at **, sk next dc, hdc in last dc, sk next dc on back, sl st in next dc. Fasten off.

Left Shoulder

Row 1: With WS facing, sk next 20 [20, 20, 26, 26, 26, 26] dc from Right Shoulder, join yarn in next dc, ch 2, *sk next 2 dc, sc shell in next dc, rep from * across, sk next dc, hdc in last dc, turn. *(25 [27, 29, 30, 32, 34, 36] shells, 2 hdc)*

Row 2: Ch 3, sk first 2 sts, *3 dc in next ch-2 sp, sk next 2 sc, rep from * across to last ch-2 sp, **dc dec** *(see Stitch Guide)* in next ch-2 sp and in last hdc, turn. *(74 [80, 86, 89, 95, 101, 107] dc)*

Row 3: Ch 2, sk first 2 sts, hdc in next dc, *sk next 2 dc, sc shell in next dc, sk next 2 dc, rep from * across, sk next dc, hdc in next dc, turn. *(23 [25, 27, 28, 30, 32, 34], 3 hdc)*

Row 4: Rep row 2. *(68 [74, 80, 86, 89, 95, 101] dc)*

Row 5: Ch 2, sk first 2 sts, *sc shell in next dc**, sk next 2 dc, rep from * across, ending last rep at **, sk next dc, hdc in last dc, turn. *(22 [24, 26, 27, 29, 31, 33] sc shells, 2 hdc)*

Row 6: Ch 3, sk first 2 sts, *3 dc in next ch-2 sp**, sk next 2 sc, rep from * across, ending last rep at **, dc in last hdc, turn.

Rows 7 & 8: Rep rows 5 and 6.

Row 9: Hold Front and Back Shoulders with RS tog, ch 2, sl st in first dc of Back, ch 1, *sk 2 dc on front, sc in next dc, sk next dc on Back, [sl st in next dc] twice, sc in same dc on Front, rep from * across, sk next dc, hdc in last dc, sl st in next dc on Back. Fasten off.

Neckline Edging

Rnd 1: Working on WS in sts and ends of rows, sk 2 dc from Back Left Shoulder, join yarn in next dc, sc shell in same dc, [sk next 2 dc, sc shell in next dc] 7 [7, 7, 9, 9, 9, 9] times, [sc shell in next row] 3 times, sk next row, [sc shell in next row] twice, sk next row, [sc shell in next row] 4 times, sk next dc, sc shell in next dc, [sk next 2 dc, sc shell in next dc] 5 [5, 5, 7, 7, 7, 7] times, sk next 2 dc, [sc shell in next row] 4 times, sk next row, [sc shell in next row] twice, sk next row, [sc shell in next row] 3 times, join in first sc. Fasten off. *(32 [32, 32, 36, 36, 36, 36] sc shells)*

Armhole Edging

Rnd 1: With WS of 1 sleeve facing and working in ends of rows, join yarn at underarm, sc shell in same row, [sk next row, sc shell in next row] 5 [6, 7, 8, 8, 9, 10] times, sc shell in each of next 17 rows, [sk next row, sc shell in next row] 5 [6, 7, 8, 8, 9, 10] times, join in first sc. Fasten off.

Rep for 2nd Armhole. ●

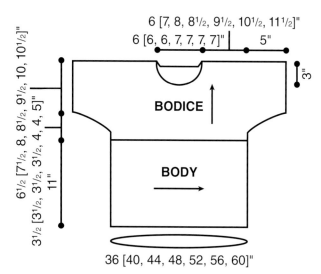

6 [7, 8, 8½, 9½, 10½, 11½]"

6 [6, 6, 7, 7, 7, 7]"

5"

3"

6½ [7½, 8, 8½, 9½, 10, 10½]"

3½ [3½, 3½, 3½, 4, 4, 5]"

11"

3½ [3½, 3½, 3½, 4, 4, 5]"

BODICE

BODY

36 [40, 44, 48, 52, 56, 60]"

Note: Arrow indicates direction of work.

Corded Shells Cowl Top

Skill Level

 INTERMEDIATE

Finished Sizes

Instructions given fit size small; changes for medium, large, X-large, 2X-large, 3X-large and 4X-large are in [ ].

Finished Measurement

Bust: 34 inches *(small)* [38 inches *(medium)*, 42 inches *(large)*, 46 inches *(X-large)*, 50 inches *(2X-large)*, 54 inches *(3X-large)*, 58 inches *(4X-large)*]

Materials

- Omega Dalia size 3 crochet cotton (3½ oz/404 yds/100g per ball): 4 [5, 5, 6, 6, 7, 8] balls #583 leaf green
- Size G/6/4mm crochet hook or size needed to obtain gauge
- Tapestry needle

Gauge

4 shells in pattern = 4 inches; 12 pattern rows = 4 inches

Pattern Notes

Weave in loose ends as work progresses.

Join with slip stitch as indicated unless otherwise stated.

Chain-3 at beginning of row counts as first double crochet unless otherwise stated.

Chain-5 at beginning of round counts as first double crochet and chain-2 unless otherwise stated.

Special Stitches

Shell: (Dc, [ch 1, dc] twice) in st indicated.

Beginning half shell (beg half shell): Ch 4, dc in st indicated.

Half shell: (Dc, ch 1, dc) in st indicated.

Front post treble crochet shell (fptr shell): (Dc, ch 1, **fptr** *(see Stitch Guide)* around center st of shell 2 rows below, ch 1, dc) in st indicated.

Beginning shell (beg shell): Ch 4, (dc, ch 1, dc) in st indicated.

Beginning front post treble crochet shell (beg fptr shell): Ch 4, fptr around center st of shell 2 rows below, ch 1, dc in st indicated.

Large shell: (Dc, [ch 2, dc] twice) in st indicated.

Beginning large front post treble crochet shell (beg large fptr shell): Ch 5 *(see Pattern Notes)*, fptr around center st of shell 2 rows below, ch 2, dc in st indicated.

Large front post treble crochet shell (large fptr shell): (Dc, ch 2, fptr around center st of shell 2 rows below, ch 2, dc) in st indicated.

Tank

Bodice Back

Row 1 (RS): Ch 74 [86, 86, 86, 98, 98, 98], sc in 2nd ch from hook, *sk next 2 chs, **shell** *(see Special Stitches)* in next ch, sk next 2 chs, sc in next ch, rep from * across, turn. *(12 [14, 14, 14, 16, 16, 16] shells)*

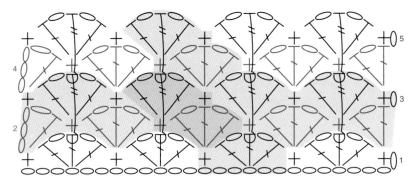

Corded Shells Cowl Top
Reduced Sample of Stitch Diagram
***Note:** Reps shown in gray.*

Row 2: Beg half shell *(see Special Stitches)* in first sc, *sk next dc and next ch sp, sc in next st, sk next ch sp and next dc**, shell in next sc, rep from * across, ending last rep at **, **half shell** *(see Special Stitches)* in last sc, turn. *(11 [13, 13, 13, 15, 15, 15] shells, 2 half shells)*

Row 3: Ch 1, sc in first dc, *sk next ch sp and next dc, **fptr shell** *(see Special Stitches)* in next sc, sk next dc and next ch sp, sc in next dc, rep from * across, turn. *(12 [14, 14, 14, 16, 16, 16] shells)*

Rows 4–15 [4–19, 4–17, 4–15, 4–17, 4–15, 4–13]: [Rep rows 2 and 3 alternately] 6 [8, 7, 6, 8, 6, 5] times.

Shape Back Armholes

Row 1 (WS): Beg shell *(see Special Stitches)* in first sc, *sk next dc and next ch sp, sc in next st, sk next ch sp and next dc, shell in next sc, rep from * across, turn. *(13 [15, 15, 15, 17, 17, 17] shells)*

Row 2 (RS): Beg shell in first dc, sk next ch sp, sc in next dc, *sk next ch sp and next dc, fptr shell in next sc, sk next dc and next ch sp, sc in next dc, rep from * across to last dc, shell in last dc, turn. *(14 [16, 16, 16, 18, 18, 18] shells)*

Row 3: Beg shell in first dc, sk next ch sp, sc in next st, *sk next ch sp and next dc, shell in next sc, sk next dc and next ch sp, sc in next st, rep from * across to last dc, shell in last dc, turn. *(15 [17, 17, 17, 19, 19, 19] shells)*

Row 4: Rep row 2. *(16 [18, 18, 18, 20, 20, 20] shells)*

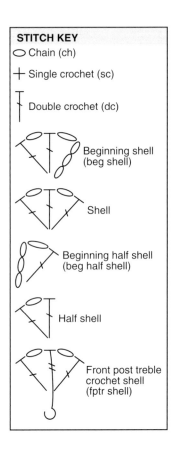

STITCH KEY
◯ Chain (ch)
+ Single crochet (sc)
⊤ Double crochet (dc)
Beginning shell (beg shell)
Shell
Beginning half shell (beg half shell)
Half shell
Front post treble crochet shell (fptr shell)

Sizes Small & Medium Only
Fasten off.

Sizes Large, X-Large, 2X-Large, 3X-Large & 4X-Large Only
Rows [5 & 6, 5–8, 5–8, 5–10, 5–12]: [Rep rows 3 and 4 alternately] [1, 2, 2, 3, 4] time(s). At end of last row, fasten off. *([20, 22, 24, 26, 28] shells at end of last row)*

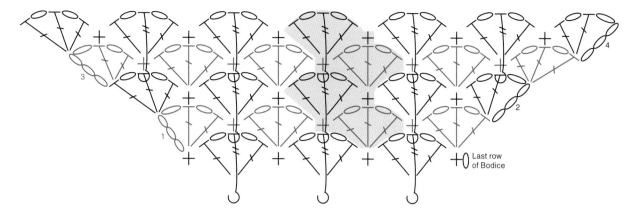

Corded Shells Cowl Top
Reduced Sample of Shape Armholes Stitch Diagram
Note: *Reps shown in gray.*

Right Shoulder

Row 1: Hold Back with WS facing and foundation ch at top, **join** *(see Pattern Notes)* yarn in 22nd [28th, 28th, 28th, 34th, 34th, 34th] ch from left edge, sc in same ch, sk next 2 chs, *shell in next ch, sk next 2 chs, sc in next ch, sk next 2 chs, rep from * across, half shell in last ch, turn. *(3 [4, 4, 4, 5, 5, 5] shells, 1 half shell)*

Note: *On following row, work fptr in corresponding dc on row 2 below of Back.*

Row 2: Ch 1, sc in first dc, sk next ch sp and next dc, *fptr shell in next sc, sk next dc and next ch sp, sc in next dc, sk next ch sp and next dc, rep from * across, dc in last sc, turn. *(3 [4, 4, 4, 5, 5, 5] shells)*

Row 3: Ch 4, sk first dc, dc in next dc *(counts as a beg half shell)*, *sk next dc and next ch sp, sc in next st, sk next ch sp and next dc**, shell in next sc, rep from * across, ending last rep at **, half shell in last sc, turn. *(2 [3, 3, 3, 4, 4, 4] shells, 2 half shells)*

Row 4: Ch 1, sc in first dc, *sk next ch sp and next dc, fptr shell in next sc, sk next dc and next ch sp, sc in next dc, rep from * across, leaving beg ch-4 unworked, turn.

Row 5: Ch 4, dc in next sc *(counts as beg half shell)*, *sk next dc and next ch sp, sc in next st, sk next ch sp and next dc**, shell in next sc, rep from * across, ending last rep at **, half shell in last sc, turn.

Row 6: Ch 1, sc in first dc, *sk next ch sp and next dc, fptr shell in next sc, sk next dc and next ch sp, sc in next dc, rep from * across, turn.

Rows 7 & 8 [7–10, 7–10, 7–10, 7–12, 7–12, 7–12]: [Rep rows 5 and 6 alternately] 1 [2, 2, 2, 3, 3, 3] time(s).

Shape Neck

Row 1: Beg shell in first sc, *sk next dc and next ch sp, sc in next st, sk next ch sp and next dc**, shell in next sc, rep from * across, ending last rep at **, half shell in last sc, turn. *(3 [4, 4, 4, 5, 5, 5] shells, 1 half shell)*

Row 2: Ch 1, sc in first dc, *sk next ch sp and next dc, *fptr shell in next sc, sk next dc and next ch sp, sc in next dc, sk next ch sp and next dc, rep from * across, shell in last dc, turn. *(4 [5, 5, 5, 6, 6, 6] shells)*

Row 3: Beg shell in first dc, sk next ch sp, *sc in next st, sk next ch sp and next dc**, shell in next sc, sk next dc and next ch sp, rep from * across, ending last rep at **, half shell in last sc, turn. *(4 [5, 5, 5, 6, 6, 6] shells, 1 half shell)*

Row 4: Rep row 2. Fasten off. *(5 [6, 6, 6, 7, 7, 7] shells)*

Left Shoulder

Row 1: With WS facing and working in foundation ch, join yarn in first ch at right edge, beg shell in same ch, [*sk next 2 chs, sc in next ch**, sk next 2 chs, shell in next ch] 3 [4, 4, 4, 5, 5, 5] times, rep from * to **, turn. *(3 [4, 4, 4, 5, 5, 5] shells, 1 half shell)*

Row 2: Ch 3 *(see Pattern Notes)*, sk first sc, *sk next dc and next ch sp, sc in next dc**, sk next ch sp and next dc, fptr shell in next sc, rep from * across, ending last rep at **, turn. *(3 [4, 4, 4, 5, 5, 5] shells)*

Row 3: Beg half shell in first sc, *sk next dc and next ch sp, sc in next st, sk next ch sp and next dc**, shell in next sc, rep from * across, ending last rep at **, half shell in last sc, turn. *(2 [3, 3, 3, 4, 4, 4] shells, 2 half shells)*

Row 4: Ch 1, sc in first dc, *sk next ch sp and next dc, fptr shell in next sc, sk next dc and next ch sp, sc in next dc, rep from * across, turn.

Rows 5–8 [5–10 5–10, 5–10, 5–12, 5–12, 5–12]: [Rep rows 3 and 4 alternately] 2 [3, 3, 3, 4, 4, 4] times.

Shape Neck
Row 1: Beg half shell in first sc, *sk next dc and next ch sp, sc in next st, sk next ch sp and next dc, shell in next sc, rep from * across, turn. *(3 [4, 4, 4, 5, 5, 5] shells, 1 half shell)*

Row 2: Beg half shell in first dc, sk next ch sp, *sc in next dc, sk next ch sp and next dc, fptr shell in next sc, sk next dc and next ch sp, rep from * across to last dc, sc in last dc, turn. *(4 [5, 5, 5, 6, 6, 6] shells, 1 half shell)*

Row 3: Beg half shell in first sc, *sk next dc and next ch sp, sc in next st, sk next ch sp** and next dc, shell in next sc, rep from * across, ending last rep at **, shell in last dc, turn. *(4 [5, 5, 5, 6, 6, 6] shells, 1 half shell)*

Row 4: Rep row 2. *(5 [6, 6, 6, 7, 7, 7] shells, 1 half shell)*

Front Bodice
Row 1: Beg half shell in first sc, *sk next dc and next ch sp, sc in next st, sk next ch sp** and next dc, shell in next sc, rep from * across, ending last rep at **, shell in last dc, ch 11, hold Front Shoulder with WS facing, working across last row, shell in next dc, sk next ch sp, sc in next st, sk next ch sp and next dc, shell in next st, ***sk next dc and next ch sp, sc in next st, sk next ch sp**** and next dc, shell in next sc, rep from *** across, ending last rep at ****, sk next dc, half shell in last sc, turn. *(10 [12, 12, 12, 14, 14, 14] shells, 2 half shells)*

Row 2: Ch 1, sc in first dc, sk next ch sp and next dc, *fptr shell in next sc, sk next dc and next ch sp, sc in next dc, sk next ch sp and next dc, rep from * across to ch-11, sk next 2 chs, shell in next ch, sk next 2 chs, sc in next ch, sk next 2 chs, shell in next ch, sk next 2 chs, sk next dc and next ch sp, sc in next dc, sk next ch sp and next dc, ***fptr shell in next sc, sk next dc and next ch sp, sc in next dc, sk next ch sp and next dc, rep from *** across, turn. *(12 [14, 14, 14, 16, 16, 16] shells)*

Row 3: Beg half shell in first sc, *sk next dc and next ch sp, sc in next st, sk next ch sp and next dc**, shell in next sc, rep from * across, ending last rep at **, half shell in last sc, turn.

Row 4: Ch 1, sc in first dc, *sk next ch sp and next dc, fptr shell in next sc, sk next dc and next ch sp, sc in next dc, rep from * across, turn.

Rows 5–14 [5–14, 5–12, 5–10, 5–10, 5–8, 5 & 6]: [Rep rows 3 and 4] 5 [5, 4, 3, 3, 2, 1] time(s).

Shape Front Armholes
Row 1 (WS): Beg shell in first sc, *sk next dc and next ch sp, sc in next st, sk next ch sp and next dc, shell in next sc, rep from * across, turn. *(13 [15, 15, 15, 17, 17, 17] shells)*

Row 2 (RS): Beg shell in first dc, sk next ch sp, *sc in next dc, sk next ch sp** and next dc, fptr shell in next sc, sk next dc and next ch sp, rep from * across, ending last rep at **, shell in last dc, turn. *(14 [16, 16, 16, 18, 18, 18] shells)*

Row 3: Beg shell in first dc, sk next ch sp, *sc in next st, sk next ch sp** and next dc, shell in next sc, sk next dc and next ch sp, rep from * across, ending last rep at **, shell in last dc, turn. *(15 [17, 17, 17, 19, 19, 19] shells)*

Row 4: Rep row 2. *(16 [18, 18, 18, 20, 20, 20] shells)*

Sizes Large, X-Large, 2X-Large, 3X-Large & 4X-Large Only

Rows [5 & 6, 5–8, 5–8, 5–10, 5–12]: [Rep rows 3 and 4] [1, 2, 2, 3, 4] time(s). *([20, 22, 24, 26, 28] shells)*

Body

Rnd 1: Now working in rnds, beg shell in first dc, sk next ch sp, *sc in next st, sk next ch sp** and next dc, shell in next sc, sk next dc and next ch sp, rep from * across, ending last rep at **, shell in last dc, ch 5, shell in first dc on WS of Back, sk next ch sp, ***sc in next st, sk next ch sp**** and next dc, shell in next sc, sk next dc and next ch sp, rep from *** across, ending last rep at ****, shell in last dc, ch 2, join with dc in first dc, turn. *(34 [38, 42, 46, 50, 54, 58] shells)*

Rnd 2: Ch 4, dc in joining dc, sk next 2 chs, *sk next dc and next ch sp, sc in next dc, sk next ch sp and next dc, fptr shell in next sc, sk next dc and next ch sp, sc in next dc, sk next ch and next dc, rep from * to ch-5 sp, sk next 2 chs, shell in next ch, sk next 2 chs, **fptr shell in next sc, sk next dc and next ch sp, sc in next dc, sk next ch and next dc, rep from ** around, dc in joining dc, ch 1, join in first dc, turn.

Rnd 3: Ch 1, sc in same st, *sk next ch sp and next dc, shell in next sc, sk next dc and next ch sp**, sc in next st, rep from * around, ending last rep at **, join, turn.

Rnd 4: Beg fptr shell *(see Special Stitches)* in first sc, *sk next dc and next ch sp, sc in next dc, sk next ch sp and next dc**, fptr shell in next sc, rep from * around, ending last rep at **, join in 3rd ch of beg ch-4, sl st in next ch sp and in next fptr, turn.

Rnds 5–30: [Rep rnds 3 and 4] 13 times.

Shape Hip

Rnd 1: Sc in first st, sk next ch sp and next dc, **large shell** *(see Special Stitches)* in next sc, sk next dc and next ch sp, sc in next st, [sk next ch sp and next dc, shell in next sc, sk next dc and next ch sp, sc in next st] 15 [17, 19, 21, 23, 25, 27] times, [sk next ch sp and next dc, large shell in next sc, sk next dc and next ch sp, sc in next st] twice, [sk next ch sp and next dc, shell in next sc, sk next dc and next ch sp, sc in next st] 15 [17, 19, 21, 23, 25, 27] times, sk next ch sp and next dc, large shell in next sc, sk next dc and next ch sp, join in first sc, turn.

Rnd 2: Beg large fptr shell *(see Special Stitches)* in first sc, sk next dc and next ch sp, sc in next dc, sk next ch sp and next dc, **large fptr shell** *(see Special Stitches)* in next sc, [sk next dc and next ch sp, sc in next dc, sk next ch sp and next dc, fptr shell in next sc] 14 [16, 18, 20, 22, 24, 26] times, [sk next dc and next ch sp, sc in next dc, sk next ch sp and next dc, large fptr shell in next sc] 3 times, [sk next dc and next ch sp, sc in next dc, sk next ch sp and next dc, fptr shell in next sc] 14 [16, 18, 20, 22, 24, 26] times, sk next dc and next ch sp, sc in next dc, sk next ch sp and next dc, large fptr shell in next sc, sk next dc and next ch sp, sc in next dc, sk next ch sp and next dc, join in 3rd ch of beg ch-5, sl st in next ch sp and in next fptr, turn.

Rnd 3: Ch 1, sc in first st, [sk next ch sp and next dc, large shell in next sc, sk next dc and next ch sp, sc in next st] twice, [sk next ch sp and next dc, shell in next sc, sk next dc and next ch sp, sc in next st] 13 [15, 17, 19, 21, 23, 25] times, [sk next ch sp and next dc, large shell in next sc, sk next dc and next ch sp, sc in next st] 4 times, [sk next ch sp and next dc, shell in next sc, sk next dc and next ch sp, sc in next st] 13 [15, 17, 19, 21, 23, 25] times, sk next ch sp and next dc, large shell in next sc, sk next dc and next ch sp, sc in next st, sk next ch sp and next dc, large shell in next sc, sk next dc and next ch sp, join in first sc, turn.

Rnd 4: Beg large fptr shell in first sc, [sk next dc and next ch sp, sc in next dc, sk next ch sp and next dc, large fptr shell in next sc] twice, [sk next dc and next ch sp, sc in next dc, sk next ch sp and next dc, fptr shell in next sc] 12 [14, 16, 18, 20, 22, 24] times, [sk next dc and next ch sp, sc in next dc, sk next ch sp and next dc, large fptr shell in next sc] 5 times, [sk next dc and next ch sp, sc in next dc, sk next ch sp and next dc, fptr shell in next sc] 12 [14, 16, 18, 20, 22, 24] times, [sk next dc and next ch sp, sc in next dc, sk next ch sp and next dc, large fptr shell in next sc] twice, sk next dc and next ch sp, sc in next dc, sk next ch sp and next dc, join in 3rd ch of beg ch-5, sl st in next ch sp and in next fptr, turn.

Rnd 5: Ch 1, sc in first st, [sk next ch sp and next dc, large shell in next sc, sk next dc and next ch sp, sc in next st] 3 times, [sk next ch sp and next dc, shell in next sc, sk next dc and next ch sp, sc in next st] 11 [13, 15, 17, 19, 21, 23] times, [sk next ch sp and next dc, large shell in next sc, sk next dc and next ch sp, sc in next st] 6 times, [sk next ch sp and next dc, shell in next sc, sk next dc and next ch sp, sc in next st] 11 [13, 15, 17, 19, 21, 23] times, [sk next ch sp and next dc, large shell in next sc, sk next dc and next ch sp, sc in next st] twice, sk next ch sp and next dc, large shell in next sc, sk next dc and next ch sp, join in first sc, turn.

Rnd 6: Beg large fptr shell in first sc, [sk next dc and next ch sp, sc in next dc, sk next ch sp and next dc, large fptr shell in next sc] 3 times, [sk next dc and next ch sp, sc in next dc, sk next ch sp and next dc, fptr shell in next sc] 10 [12, 14, 16, 18, 20, 22] times, [sk next dc and next ch sp, sc in next dc, sk next ch sp and next dc, large fptr shell in next sc] 7 times, [sk next dc and next ch sp, sc in next dc, sk next ch sp and next dc, fptr shell in next sc] 10 [12, 14, 16, 18, 20, 22] times, [sk next dc and next ch sp, sc in next dc, sk next ch sp and next dc, large fptr shell in next sc] 3 times, sk next dc and next ch sp, sc in next dc, sk next ch sp and next dc, join, sl st in next ch sp and in next fptr, join in 3rd ch of beg ch-5, turn.

Rnd 7: Ch 1, sc in first st, [sk next ch sp and next dc, large shell in next sc, sk next dc and next ch sp, sc in next st] 4 times, [sk next ch sp and next dc, shell in next sc, sk next dc and next ch sp, sc in next st] 9 [11, 13, 15, 17, 19, 21] times, [sk next ch sp and next dc, large shell in next sc, sk next dc and next ch sp, sc in next st] 8 times, [sk next ch sp and next dc, shell in next sc, sk next dc and next ch sp, sc in next st] 9 [11, 13, 15, 17, 19, 21] times, [sk next ch sp and next dc, large shell in next sc, sk next dc and next ch sp, sc in next st] 3 times, sk next ch sp and next dc, large shell in next sc, sk next dc and next ch sp, join in first sc, turn.

Rnd 8: Beg large fptr shell in first sc, [sk next dc and next ch sp, sc in next dc, sk next ch sp and next dc, large fptr shell in next sc] 4 times, [sk next dc and next ch sp, sc in next dc, sk next ch sp and next dc, fptr shell in next sc] 9 [11, 13, 15, 17, 19, 21] times, [sk next dc and next ch sp, sc in next dc, sk next ch sp and next dc, large fptr shell in next sc] 8 times, [sk next dc and next ch sp, sc in next dc, sk next ch sp and next dc, fptr shell in next sc] 9 [11, 13, 15, 17, 19, 21] times, [sk next dc and next ch sp, sc in next dc, sk next ch sp and next dc, large fptr shell in next sc] 3 times, sk next dc and next ch sp, sc in next dc, sk next ch sp and next dc, join in 3rd ch of beg ch-5, sl st in next ch sp and in next fptr, turn.

Rnds 9–20: [Rep rnds 7 and 8] 6 times, ending last rnd with sl st in next ch-1 sp, do not turn.

Rnd 21: Ch 1, 2 sc in same ch sp as beg ch-1, *fpdc *(see Stitch Guide)* around next tr, 2 sc in next ch sp, sk next dc, sc in next sc, sk next dc, 2 sc in next ch sp, rep from * around, join in first sc, do not turn.

Rnd 22: Ch 1, **reverse sc** *(see Stitch Guide)* in each sc around, join in first reverse sc. Fasten off.

Cowl

Rnd 1: With WS facing, working in ch sts around necklines and in ends of rows, join yarn in ch at base of last sc in row 1 of Left Shoulder on back neckline, ch 1, sc in same ch as beg ch-1, [sk next 2 chs, shell in next ch, sk next 2 chs, sc in next ch] 5 times, *[shell in next row, sc in next row] 5 [6, 6, 6, 7, 7, 7] times*, sk next row, shell in next row, sk next 2 chs, sc in next ch, sk next 2 chs, shell in next ch, sk next 2 chs, sc in next ch, sk next 2 chs, shell in next row, sk next row, rep from * to *, join in first sc, turn. *(18 [20, 20, 20, 22, 22, 22] shells)*

Rnd 2: Beg fptr shell in first sc, *[sk next dc and next ch sp, sc in next dc, sk next ch sp and next dc, shell in next sc] 5 [6, 6, 6, 7, 7, 7] times*, [sk next dc and next ch sp, sc in next dc, sk next ch sp and next dc, fptr shell in next sc] twice, rep from * to *, [sk next dc and next ch sp, sc in next dc, sk next ch sp and next dc, fptr shell in next sc] 5 times, join in 3rd ch of beg ch-4, sl st in next ch sp and in next fptr, turn.

Rnd 3: Ch 1, sc in first st, *sk next ch sp and next dc, fptr shell in next sc, sk next dc and next ch sp**, sc in next st, rep from * around, ending last rep at **, join in first sc, turn.

Rnd 4: Beg fptr shell in first sc, [sk next dc and next ch sp, sc in next st, sk next ch sp and next dc, fptr shell in next sc] 3 times, [sk next dc and next ch sp, sc in next st, sk next ch sp and next dc, large fptr shell in next sc] 7 [8, 8, 8, 9, 9, 9] times, [sk next dc and next ch sp, sc in next st, sk next ch sp and next dc, fptr shell in next sc] 7 [8, 8, 8, 9, 9, 9] times, sk next dc and next ch sp, sc in next st, sk next ch sp and next dc, join in 3rd ch of beg ch-4, sl st in next ch sp and in next fptr, turn.

Rnd 5: Ch 1, sc in first st, [sk next ch sp and next dc, fptr shell in next sc, sk next dc and next ch sp, sc in next st] 5 times, [sk next ch sp and next dc, large fptr shell in next sc, sk next dc and next ch sp, sc in next st] 12 times, sk next ch sp and next dc, fptr shell in next sc, sk next dc and next ch sp, join in first sc, turn.

Rnd 6: Beg large fptr shell in first sc, *sk next dc and next ch sp, sc in next st, sk next ch sp and next dc**, large fptr shell in next sc, rep from * around, ending last rep at **, join in 3rd ch of beg ch-5, sl st in next ch sp and in next fptr, turn.

Rnd 7: Ch 1, sc in first st, *sk next ch sp and next dc, large fptr shell in next sc, sk next dc and next ch sp**, sc in next st, rep from * around, ending last rep at **, join in first sc, turn.

Rnds 8–15: [Rep rnds 6 and 7] 4 times.

Rnd 16: Beg large fptr shell in first sc, *ch 1, sk next dc and next ch sp, sc in next st, ch 1, sk next ch sp and next dc**, large fptr shell in next sc, rep from * around, ending last rep at **, join in 3rd ch of beg ch-5, sl st in next ch sp and in next fptr, turn.

Rnd 17: Ch 1, sc in first st, *ch 1, sk next ch sp and next dc, large fptr shell in next sc, ch 1, sk next dc and next ch sp**, sc in next st, rep from * around, ending last rep at **, join in first sc, turn.

Rnds 18–25: [Rep rnds 16 and 17] 4 times.

Rnd 26: Beg large fptr shell in first sc, *ch 2, sk next dc and next ch sp, sc in next st, ch 2, sk next ch sp and next dc**, large fptr shell in next sc, rep from * around, ending last rep at **, join in 3rd ch of beg ch-5, sl st in next ch sp and in next fptr, turn.

Rnd 27: Ch 1, sc in first st, *ch 2, sk next ch sp and next dc, large fptr shell in next sc, ch 2, sk next dc and next ch sp**, sc in next st, rep from * around, ending last rep at **, join in first sc, turn.

Rnd 28: Rep rnd 26, ending with sl st in next ch sp, do not turn.

Rnd 29: Ch 1, 2 sc in same sp as beg ch-1, *sk next dc, sc in next ch-2 sp, fpdc around next tr 2 rows below, sc in next ch-2 sp, sk next dc, 2 sc in next ch-2 sp, sc in next tr**, 2 sc in next ch-2 sp, rep from * around, ending last rep at **, join in first sc, do not turn.

Rnd 30: Ch 1, reverse sc in each st around, join in first reverse sc. Fasten off.

Armhole Edging
Rnd 1: Hold piece with RS facing, working in ch sps and in ends of rows around 1 Armhole, join yarn at bottom of Armhole, sc in same sp, [2 sc in next row] 3 times, sc in each of next 42 [49, 49, 49, 53, 53, 53] rows, 2 sc in each of next 3 rows, join in first sc, ch 1, do not turn. *(55 [61, 61, 61, 65, 65, 65] sc)*

Rnd 2: Ch 1, reverse sc in each sc around, join in first reverse sc. Fasten off.

Rep around 2nd Armhole. ●

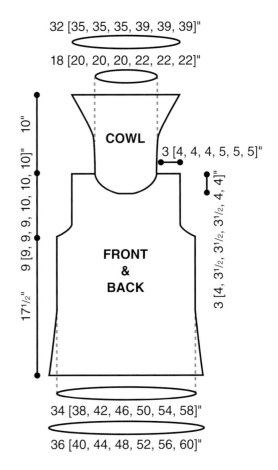

32 [35, 35, 35, 39, 39, 39]"

18 [20, 20, 20, 22, 22, 22]"

COWL

3 [4, 4, 4, 5, 5, 5]"

3 [4, 3½, 3½, 3½, 4, 4]"

FRONT & BACK

10"

9 [9, 9, 10, 10, 10]"

17½"

34 [38, 42, 46, 50, 54, 58]"

36 [40, 44, 48, 52, 56, 60]"

Driftwood Blossom Tee

Skill Level

 INTERMEDIATE

Finished Sizes

Instructions given fit size small; changes for medium, large, X-large, 2X-large, 3X-large and 4X-large are in [ ].

Finished Measurement

Bust: 35 inches *(small)* [40 inches *(medium)*, 45 inches *(large)*, 50 inches *(X-large)*, 55 inches *(2X-large)*, 60 inches *(3X-large)*, 65 inches *(4X-large)*]

Materials

- Omega Dalia size 3 crochet cotton (3½ oz/404 yds/100g per ball):
  2 [3, 3, 4, 4, 5, 5] balls #518 ecru
  2 [2, 3, 3, 4, 4, 5] balls #525 light brown
  Sizes G/6/4mm and 7/4.5mm crochet hooks or sizes needed to obtain gauge
- Stitch marker
- Tapestry needle

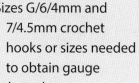

Gauge

With smaller hook: 4 pattern reps and 12 rows = 4 inches

With larger hook: Motif = 2½ inches square; 4 pattern reps and 12 rows = 5 inches

Pattern Notes

Weave in loose ends as work progresses.

Join with slip stitch as indicated unless otherwise stated.

Chain-3 at beginning of round counts as first double crochet unless otherwise stated.

Chain-5 at beginning of row counts as first double crochet and chain-2 unless otherwise stated.

Chain-3 at beginning of row counts as first double crochet unless otherwise stated.

Use larger hook for Motifs and Body; use smaller hook from Bodice onward.

Special Stitches

Shell: (Sc, ch 2, 2 dc) in space indicated.

Beginning shell (beg shell): Sc in first dc, ch 2, 2 dc in first ch-2 sp as indicated.

Band

Motif

Make 14 [16, 18, 20, 22, 24, 26].

Rnd 1 (RS): With larger hook and light brown, ch 4, (2 dc, [ch 2, 3 dc] 3 times) in 4th ch from hook (beg 3 sk chs count as a double crochet), ch 2, **join** (see Pattern Notes) in 3rd ch of beg 3 sk chs. Fasten off. (12 dc)

Rnd 2: Join ecru in last ch-2 sp made, **ch 3** (see Pattern Notes), 2 dc in same sp, [ch 1, (3 dc, ch 3, 3 dc) in next ch-3 sp] 3 times, ch 1, 3 dc in next ch-3 sp, ch 3, join in 3rd ch of beg ch-3. Fasten off. (24 dc)

Motifs Joining

Rnd 3: Join light brown in last ch-3 sp of any Motif, ch 3, 2 dc in same sp, [ch 1, 3 dc in next ch-1 sp, ch 1, (3 dc, ch 3, 3 dc) in next ch-3 sp] twice, ch 1, 3 dc in next ch-1 sp, ch 1, *3 dc in next ch-3 sp, ch 3, 3 dc in last ch-3 sp made on new Motif, sl st in ch-1 sp on previous Motif, 3 dc in next ch-1 sp on working Motif, sl st in next ch-1 sp on previous Motif, 3 dc in next ch-3 sp of working Motif, ch 1, sl st in corresponding ch-3 sp on previous Motif, ch 1, 3 dc in same ch-3 sp of working Motif, ch 1, 3 dc in next ch-1 sp, ch 1**,

(3 dc, ch 3, 3 dc) in next ch-3 sp, ch 1, ch-3 sp, ch 1, rep from * around rem Motifs, ending last rep on last Motif at **, 3 dc in next ch-3 sp, ch 1 *(mark this ch-1 sp for Bodice joining)*, sl st in corresponding ch-3 sp on first Motif, ch 1, 3 dc in same ch-3 sp on working Motif, sl st in corresponding ch-1 sp on first Motif, 3 dc in next ch-1 sp on working Motif, sl st in corresponding ch-1 sp on first Motif, 3 dc in next ch-3 sp on working Motif, ch 1, join with dc in 3rd ch of beg ch-3.

Rnd 4: Ch 1, 3 dc in same ch-3 sp on last Motif as last 3 dc made, [ch 1, 3 dc in next ch-1 sp, ch 1, 3 dc in next ch-3 sp, ch 1, sl st in next joining ch sp, ch 1, 3 dc in next ch-3 sp] 13 [15, 17, 19, 21, 23, 25] times, ch 1, 3 dc in next ch-1 sp, ch 1, 3 dc in next ch-3 sp, ch 1, sl st in next joining ch sp, turn. *(504 [576, 648, 720, 792, 864, 936] dc)*

Body

Rnd 1 (WS): Ch 3, dc in first ch-3 sp, *sk next 3 dc, sc in next ch-1 sp, ch 3, sk next 3 dc, **shell** *(see Special Stitches)* in next ch-1 sp, sk next 3 dc, sc in next ch-3 sp, ch 3**, shell in next ch-3 sp, rep from * around, ending last rep at **, sc in same ch-3 sp as beg ch-3, join with hdc in 3rd ch of beg ch-3 *(counts as last ch sp)*, turn. *(28 [32, 36, 40, 44, 48, 52] shells, 28 [32, 36, 40, 44, 48, 52] ch-3 sps)*

Rnd 2: Ch 3, dc in first ch-2 sp, *sk next sc, sc in next ch-3 sp, ch 3, sk next sc and next 2 dc**, shell in next ch-2 sp, rep from * around, ending last rep at **, sc in same sp as beg ch-3, join with hdc in 3rd ch of beg ch-3, turn.

Rnd 3: Ch 3, dc in sp formed by joining hdc, *sk next sc, sc in next ch-3 sp, ch 3, sk next sc and next 2 dc**, shell in next ch-2 sp, rep from * around, ending last rep at **, sc in same sp as beg ch-3, join with hdc in 3rd ch of beg ch-3, turn.

Rnds 4–35 [4–35, 4–33, 4–35, 4–33, 4–33, 4–33]: Rep rnd 3.

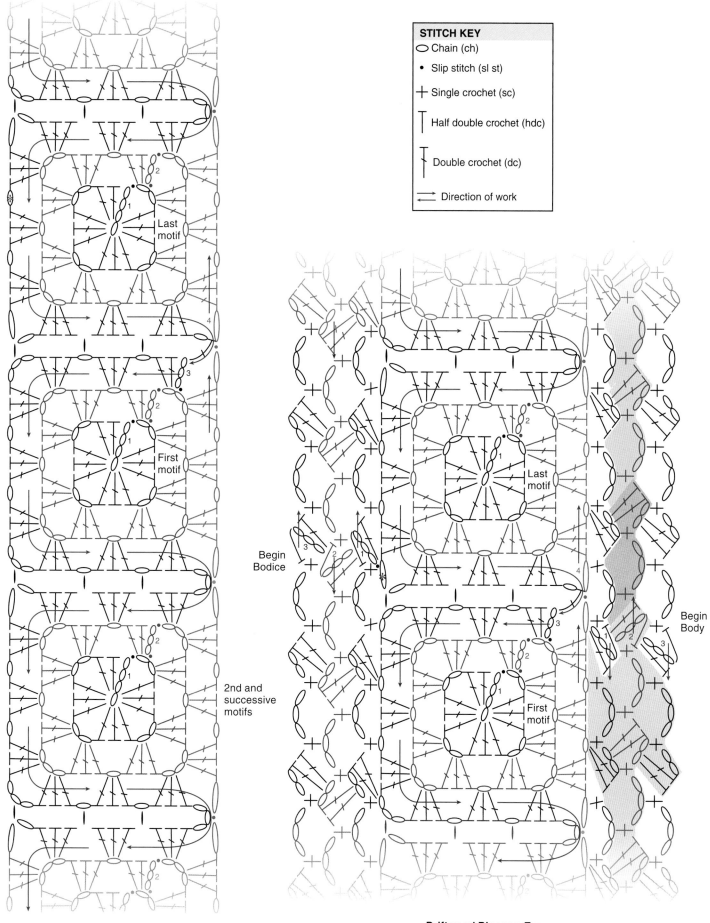

STITCH KEY
- Chain (ch)
- Slip stitch (sl st)
- Single crochet (sc)
- Half double crochet (hdc)
- Double crochet (dc)
- Direction of work

Last motif

First motif

2nd and successive motifs

Begin Bodice

Last motif

First motif

Begin Body

Driftwood Blossom Tee
Reduced Sample of Band Stitch Diagram

Driftwood Blossom Tee
Reduced Sample of Body Stitch Diagram
Note: Reps shown in gray.

Rnd 36 [36, 34, 36, 34, 34, 34]: Ch 3, dc in sp formed by joining hdc, *sk next sc, shell in next ch-3 sp, sk next sc and next 2 dc**, shell in next ch-2 sp, rep from * around, ending last rep at **, sc in same sp as beg ch-3, ch 2, join in 3rd ch of beg ch-3. Fasten off. *(56 [64, 72, 80, 88, 96, 104] shells)*

Bodice

Rnd 1 (WS): With smaller hook, join ecru on WS of opposite edge of Band in marked ch sp, ch 3, dc in same sp, *sk next 3 dc, sc in next ch-1 sp, ch 3, sk next 3 dc, shell in next ch-1 sp, sk next 3 dc, sc in next ch sp, ch 3**, shell in next ch sp, rep from * around, ending last rep at **, sc in same sp as beg ch-3, join with hdc in 3rd ch of beg ch-3 *(counts as last ch sp)*, turn. *(28 [32, 36, 40, 44, 48, 52] shells, 28 [32, 36, 40, 44, 48, 52] ch-3 sps)*

Note: Mark last ch sp made and move marker up as work progresses.

Rnd 2: Ch 3, dc in first ch-2 sp, *sk next sc, sc in next ch-3 sp, ch 3 **, shell in next ch-2 sp, rep from * around, ending last rep at **, sc in same sp as beg ch-3, join with hdc in 3rd ch of beg ch-3, turn.

Rnds 3–6 [3–6, 3–6, 3–4, 3–4, 3–4, 3–4]: [Rep rnd 2] 4 [4, 4, 2, 2, 2, 2] times. Fasten off.

Back & Sleeves

Row 1 (WS): Ch 51 [51, 43, 43, 35, 35, 35], with WS facing, shell in marked ch sp, [sk next sc, sc in next ch-3 sp, ch 3, sk next sc and next 2 dc, shell in next ch-2 sp] 13 [15, 17, 19, 21, 23, 25] times, sk next sc, sc in next ch-3 sp, ch 47 [47, 39, 39, 31, 31, 31], turn. *(14 [16, 18, 20, 22, 24, 26] shells, 13 [15, 17, 19, 21, 23, 25] ch-3 sps)*

Row 2 (RS): Shell in 2nd ch from hook, [sk next 3 chs, sc in next ch, ch 3, sk next 3 chs, shell in next ch] 5 [5, 4, 4, 3, 3, 3] times, sk next 3 chs, sc in next ch, ch 3, sk next ch, next sc and next 2 dc, [shell in next ch-2 sp, sk next sc, sc in next ch-3 sp, ch 3, sk next sc and next 2 dc] 13 [15, 17, 19, 21, 23, 25] times, shell in next ch-2 sp, sk next sc, sk next 2 chs, [sc in next ch, ch 3, sk next 3 ch, shell in next ch, sk next 3 ch] 6 [6, 5, 5, 4, 4, 4] times, sc in next ch, turn. *(26 [28, 28, 30, 30, 32, 34] shells, 25 [27, 27, 29, 29, 31, 31] ch-3 sps)*

Row 3: Ch 5 *(see Pattern Notes)*, sk next 2 dc, *shell in next ch-2 sp, sk next sc**, sc in next ch-3 sp, ch 3, sk next sc and next 2 dc, rep from * across to last 5 [5, 4, 4, 3, 3, 3] ch-3 sps, ending last rep at **, sk next ch, sc in next ch, leaving rem sts unworked, turn. *(21 [23, 24, 26, 29, 29, 31] shells, 20 [22, 23, 25, 28, 28, 30] ch-3 sps)*

Row 4: Ch 3 *(see Pattern Notes)*, sk next 2 dc, *shell in next ch-2 sp, sk next sc**, sc in next ch-3 sp, ch 3, sk next sc and next 2 dc, rep from * across to last 5 [5, 4, 4, 3, 3, 3] ch-3 sps, ending last rep at **, sk next ch, sc in next ch, leaving rem sts unworked, turn. *(16 [18, 20, 22, 26, 26, 28] shells, 15 [17, 19, 21, 25, 25, 27] ch-3 sps)*

Row 5: Ch 3, sk next 2 dc, *shell in next ch-2 sp, sk next sc**, sc in next ch-3 sp, ch 3, sk next sc and next 2 dc, rep from * across, ending last rep at **, sk next ch-3 sp, sc in next sc 2 rows below, ch 3, sk next sc and next 2 dc 3 rows below, shell in next ch-2 sp, sk next sc, sk next ch, sc in next ch, turn. *(17 [19, 21, 23, 27, 27, 29] shells, 16 [18, 20, 22, 26, 26, 27] ch-3 sps)*

Sizes Small & Medium Only

Row 6: Ch 3, sk next 2 dc, *shell in next ch-2 sp, sk next sc**, sc in next ch-3 sp, ch 3, sk next sc and next 2 dc, rep from * across, ending last rep at **, sk next ch-3 sp, sc in next sc 2 rows below, ch 3, sk next sc and next 2 dc on row 3 below, shell in next ch-2 sp, sk next sc, sk next ch, sc in next ch, turn. *(18 [20] shells, 17 [19] ch-3 sps)*

Row 7: Ch 3, sk next 2 dc, *shell in next ch-2 sp, sk next sc**, sc in next ch-3 sp, ch 3, sk next sc and next 2 dc, rep from * across, ending last rep at **, sk next ch-3 sp, sc in next sc 2 rows below, ch 3, sk next sc and next 2 dc on row 2 below, shell in next ch-2 sp, sk next sc, sk next ch, sc in next ch, turn. *(19 [21] shells, 18 [20] ch-3 sps)*

Row 8: Ch 3, sk next 2 dc, *shell in next ch-2 sp, sk next sc**, sc in next ch-3 sp, ch 3, sk next sc and next 2 dc, rep from * across, ending last rep at **, sk next ch-3, sc in next sc 2 rows below, ch 3, sk next sc and next 2 dc on row 3 below, shell in next ch-2 sp, sk next sc, sk next ch, sc in next ch, turn. *(20 [22] shells, 19 [21] ch-3 sps)*

Row 9: Ch 3, sk next 2 dc, *shell in next ch-2 sp, sk next sc**, sc in next ch-3 sp, ch 3, sk next sc and next 2 dc, rep from * across, ending last rep at **, sk next ch-3, sc in next sc 2 rows below, ch 3, sk next sc and next 2 dc on row 2 below, shell in next ch-2 sp, sk next sc, sk next ch, sc in next ch, turn. *(21 [23] shells, 20 [22] ch-3 sps)*

Row 10: Ch 3, sk next 2 dc, *shell in next ch-2 sp, sk next sc**, sc in next ch-3 sp, ch 3, sk next sc and next 2 dc, rep from * across, ending last rep at **, sk next ch-3, sc in next sc 2 rows below, ch 3, sk next sc and next 2 dc on row 3 below, shell in next ch-2 sp, sk next sc, sk next ch, sc in next ch, turn. *(22 [24] shells, 21 [23] ch-3 sps)*

Sizes Large & X-Large Only

Row [6]: Ch 3, sk next 2 dc, *shell in next ch-2 sp, sk next sc**, sc in next ch-3 sp, ch 3, sk next sc and next 2 dc, rep from * across, ending last rep at **, sk next ch-3, sc in next sc 2 rows below, ch 3, sk next sc and next 2 dc on row 3 below, shell in next ch-2 sp, sk next sc, sk next ch, sc in next ch, turn. *([22, 24] shells, [21, 23] ch-3 sps)*

Row [7]: Ch 3, sk next 2 dc, *shell in next ch-2 sp, sk next sc**, sc in next ch-3 sp, ch 3, sk next sc and next 2 dc, rep from * across, ending last rep at **, sk next ch-3, sc in next sc 2 rows below, ch 3, sk next sc and next 2 dc on row 2 below, shell in next ch-2 sp, sk next sc, sk next ch, sc in next ch, turn. *([23, 25] shells, [22, 24] ch-3 sps)*

Row [8]: Ch 3, sk next 2 dc, *shell in next ch-2 sp, sk next sc**, sc in next ch-3 sp, ch 3, sk next sc and next 2 dc, rep from * across, ending last rep at **, sk next ch-3, sc in next sc 2 rows below, ch 3, sk next sc and next 2 dc on row 3 below, shell in next ch-2 sp, sk next sc, sk next ch, sc in next ch, turn. *([24, 26] shells, [23, 25] ch-3 sps)*

Sizes 2X-Large, 3X-Large & 4X-Large Only

Row [6]: Ch 3, sk next 2 dc, *shell in next ch-2 sp, sk next sc**, sc in next ch-3 sp, ch 3, sk next sc and next 2 dc, rep from * across, ending last rep at **, sk next ch-3, sc in next sc 2 rows below, ch 3, sk next sc and next 2 dc on row 3 below, shell in next ch-2 sp, sk next sc, sk next ch, sc in next ch, turn. *[28, 28, 30] shells, [27, 27, 29] ch-3 sps)*

All Sizes

Row 11 [11, 9, 9, 7, 7, 7]: Ch 3, sk next 2 dc, *shell in next ch-2 sp, sk next sc**, sc in next ch-3 sp, ch 3, sk next sc and next 2 dc**, rep from * across, ending last rep at **, sk next ch-3, sc in next sc 2 rows below, ch 3, sk next sc and next 2 dc on row 2 below, shell in next ch-2 sp, sk next sc, sc in next ch-3 sp, ch 3, sk next sc and next 2 dc, sc in next ch-2 sp, ch 2, dc in last sc, turn. *(23 [25, 25, 26, 30, 30, 31] shells 22 [24, 24, 25, 29, 29, 30] ch-3 sps)*

Row 12 [12, 10, 10, 8, 8, 8]: Ch 1, **beg shell** *(see Special Stitches)* in first dc and next ch-2 sp, *sk next sc, sc in next ch-3 sp, ch 3, sk next sc and next 2 dc, shell in next ch-2 sp**, rep from * across, sk next sc and next ch-3, sc in next sc 2 rows below, ch 3, sk next sc and next 2 dc on row 3 below, shell in next ch-2 sp, sk next sc, sc in next ch-3 sp, ch 3, sk next sc and next 2 dc, shell in next ch-2 sp, sk next sc and next 2 chs, sc in last dc, turn. *(26 [28, 28, 29, 33, 33, 34] shells, 25 [27, 27, 28, 32, 32, 33] ch-3 sps)*

Row 13 [13, 11, 11, 9, 9, 9]: Ch 5, sk next 2 dc, *shell in next ch-2 sp, sk next sc, sc in next ch-3 sp, ch 3, sk next sc and next 2 dc, rep from * across, sc in next ch-2 sp, ch 2, dc in last sc, turn.

Row 14 [14, 12, 12, 10, 10, 10]: Ch 1, beg shell, *sk next sc, sc in next ch-3 sp, ch 3, sk next sc and next 2 dc, shell in next ch-2 sp, rep from * across, sk next sc and next 2 chs, sc in last dc, turn.

Rows 15–28 [15–30, 13–30, 13–32, 11–32, 11–34, 11–36]: [Rep last 2 rows alternately] 7 [8, 9, 10, 11, 12, 13] times. At end of last row, fasten off.

Front Armhole Shaping

Row 1: Hold Back with WS facing, working in unworked side of foundation ch, join ecru in first ch at right edge, ch 1, shell in same ch, [sk next 3 chs, sc in next ch, ch 3, sk next 3 chs, shell in next ch] 5 [5, 4, 4, 3, 3, 3] times, sk next 3 chs, sc in next ch, ch 3, working across last rnd of Bodice Front, [sk next sc and next 2 dc, shell in next ch-2 sp, sk next sc, sc in next ch-3 sp, ch 3] 14 [16, 18, 20, 22, 24, 26] times, sk next sc and next foundation ch, *shell in next ch, sk next 3 chs, sc in next ch**, ch 3, sk next 3 chs, rep from * across, ending last rep at **, turn. *(26 [28, 28, 30, 30, 32, 34] shells, 25 [27, 27, 29, 29, 31, 31] ch-3 sps)*

Rows 2–11 [2–11, 2–9, 2–9, 2–7, 2–7, 2–7]: Rep rows 3–12 [3–12, 3–10, 3–10, 3–8, 3–8, 3–8] of Back.

Left Front

Row 1: Ch 5, sk next 2 dc, [shell in next ch-2 sp, sk next sc, sc in next ch-3 sp, ch 3, sk next sc and next 2 dc] 11 [12, 12, 13, 13, 14, 15] times, shell in next ch-2 sp, sk next sc, sc in next ch-3 sp, ch 1, sk next sc and next 2 dc, dc in next ch-2 sp, leaving rem sts unworked, turn. *(12 [13, 13, 14, 14, 15, 16] shells, 11 [12, 12, 13, 13, 14, 15] ch-3 sps)*

Row 2: *Ch 3, sk next sc and next 2 dc, shell in next ch-2 sp, sk next sc**, sc in next ch-3 sp, rep from * across, ending last rep at **, sk next 2 chs, sc in last dc, turn.

Row 3: Ch 5, sk next 2 dc, *shell in next ch-2 sp, sk next sc, sc in next ch-3 sp**, ch 3, sk next sc and next 2 dc, rep from * across to last shell, ending last rep at **, ch 1, sk next sc and next 2 dc, dc in next ch-2 sp, turn. *(11 [12, 12, 13, 13, 14, 15] shells, 10 [11, 11, 12, 12, 13, 14] ch-3 sps)*

Rows 4 & 5: [Rep rows 2 and 3]. *(10 [11, 11, 12, 12, 13, 14] shells, 9 [10, 10, 11, 11, 12, 13] ch-3 sps at end of last row)*

Row 6: Rep row 2.

Row 7: Ch 5, sk next 2 dc, *shell in next ch-2 sp, sk next sc, sc in next ch-3 sp, ch 3, sk next sc and next 2 dc, rep from * across to last ch-2 sp, sc in last ch-2 sp, ch 2, dc in last sc, turn. *(9 [10, 10, 11, 11, 12, 13] shells, 9 [10, 10, 11, 11, 12, 13] ch-3 sps)*

Row 8: Ch 1, beg shell, *sk next sc, sc in next ch-3 sp, ch 3, sk next sc and next 2 dc, shell in next ch-2 sp, rep from * across to last sc, sk last sc and next 2 chs, sc in last dc, turn. *(10 [11, 11, 12, 12, 13, 14] shells, 9 [10, 10, 11, 11, 12, 13] ch-3 sps)*

Rows 9–18 [9–20, 9–22, 9–24, 9–26, 9–28, 9–30]: [Rep rows 7 and 8 alternately] 5 [6, 7, 8, 9, 10, 11] times.

Row 19 [21, 23, 25, 27, 29, 31]: Ch 3, sl st in first sc of corresponding Back sleeve, ch 2, sk next 2 dc on Front, *sc in next ch-2 sp, sl st in next ch-2 sp of Back**, 2 dc in same ch-2 sp of Front, sk next sc, sc in next ch-3 sp, sl st in next ch-3 sp of Back, ch 2, sk next sc and next 2 dc, rep from * across, ending last rep at **, 2 dc in last sc of Front, sl st in next ch-3 sp of Back, fasten off.

Right Front

Row 1: Hold Bodice with RS facing, working in last row of Bodice, join ecru in first ch-2 sp, ch 1, shell in same sp, *sk next sc, sc in next ch-3 sp, ch 3, sk next sc and next 2 dc, shell in next ch-2 sp, rep from * across to last sc, sk last sc and next 2 chs, sc in last dc, turn. *(12 [13, 13, 14, 14, 15, 16] shells, 12 [13, 13, 14, 14, 15, 16] ch-3 sps)*

Row 2: Ch 1, beg shell, *sk next sc, sc in next ch-3 sp**, ch 3, sk next sc and next 2 dc, shell in next ch-2 sp, rep from * across, ending last rep at **, sk next sc and next 2 dc, ch 1, dc in last ch-2 sp, turn.

Row 3: *Ch 3, sk next sc and next 2 dc**, shell in next ch-2 sp, sk next sc, sc in next ch-3 sp, rep from * across, ending last rep at **, sc in next ch-2 sp, ch 2, dc in last sc, ch 1, turn. *(10 [11, 11, 12, 12, 13, 14] shells, 11 [12, 12, 13, 13, 14, 15] ch-3 sps)*

Rows 4 & 5: Rep rows 2 and 3. *(10 [11, 11, 12, 12, 13, 14] shells, 10 [11, 11, 12, 12, 13, 14] ch-3 sps at end of last row)*

Row 6: Rep row 2.

Row 7: Ch 5, sk next 2 dc, *shell in next ch-2 sp, sk next sc, sc in next ch-3 sp, ch 3, sk next sc and next 2 dc, rep from * across to last ch-2 sp, sc in last ch-2 sp, ch 2, dc in last sc, turn. *(9 [10, 10, 11, 11, 12, 13] shells, 10 [11, 11, 12, 12, 13, 14] ch-3 sps)*

Row 8: Ch 1, beg shell, *sk next sc, sc in next ch-3 sp, ch 3, sk next sc and next 2 dc, shell in next ch-2 sp, rep from * across to last sc, sk last sc and next 2 chs, sc in last dc, turn.

Rows 9–18 [9–20, 9–22, 9–24, 9–26, 9–28, 9–30]: [Rep rows 7 and 8 alternately] 5 [6, 7, 8, 9, 10, 11] times.

Row 19 [21, 23, 25, 27, 29, 31]: Ch 3, sk 6 shells on Back, sl st in next ch-3 sp on Back, ch 2, sk next 2 dc on Front, *sc in next ch-2 sp, sl st in next ch-2 sp on Back**, 2 dc in same ch-2 sp on Front, sk next sc, sc in next ch-3 sp, sl st in next ch-3 sp on Back, ch 2, sk next sc and next 2 dc, rep from * across, ending last rep at **, dc in last sc on Front, sl st in last sc on Back. Fasten off.

Neck Edging

With RS facing and working in ends of rows and in sts around neckline, join ecru in ch-3 sp on Back at left shoulder, ch 1, shell in same sp, *[sk next row, shell in next row] 6 [7, 8, 9, 10, 11, 12] times*, shell in each of next 12 rows, rep from * to *, shell in next row, [shell in next ch-2 sp, sc in next ch-3 sp] 6 times, join in first sc. Fasten off. *(32 [36, 40, 44, 48, 52, 60] shells)*

Sleeve Edging

With RS facing and working in ends of rows around Sleeve Edge, join ecru in foundation ch at underarm, ch 1, shell in same sp, shell in next row, *sk next row, shell in next row, rep from * around, join in first sc. Fasten off. *(20 [22, 24, 26, 28, 30, 32] shells)*

Rep for 2nd armhole. ●

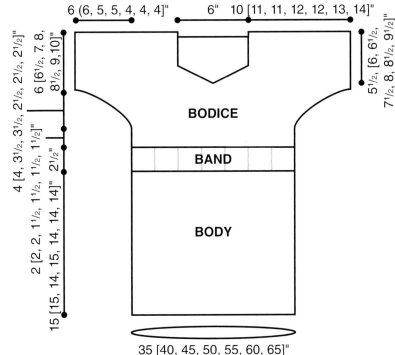

Eyelet Dream Tank

Skill Level

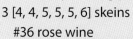 INTERMEDIATE

Finished Sizes

Instructions given fit size small; changes for medium, large, X-large, 2X-large, 3X-large and 4X-large are in [ ].

Finished Measurement

Bust: 35½ inches *(small)* [39 inches *(medium)*, 42½ inches *(large)*, 46¼ inches *(X-large)*, 53¼ inches *(2X-large)*, 56¾ inches *(3X-large)*, 60¼ inches *(4X-large)*]

Materials

- Omega Mimosa fine (sport) weight cotton/rayon yarn (3½ oz/ 240 yds/100g per skein): 3 [4, 4, 5, 5, 5, 6] skeins #36 rose wine
- Size 7/4.5mm crochet hook or size needed to obtain gauge
- Tapestry needle

Gauge

18 sts = 4 inches; 8 pattern rows = 4 inches

Pattern Notes

When working in ends of rows in round 1 of Bodice, work into stitches rather than over them for a finer result. For remaining rounds and rows of Bodice, work into chain-1 spaces.

The pattern shifts in the last 2 rows of front shoulders to mirror preceding rows and match back neckline.

Weave in loose ends as work progresses.

Chain-3 at beginning of row counts as first double crochet unless otherwise stated.

Chain-4 at beginning of row counts as first double crochet and chain-1 unless otherwise stated.

Join with slip stitch as indicated unless otherwise stated.

Chain-3 at beginning of round counts as first double crochet unless otherwise stated.

Chain-4 at beginning of round counts as first double crochet and chain-1 unless otherwise stated.

Tank

Body Front

Row 1 (RS): Ch 33, dc in 4th ch from hook *(beg 3 sk chs count as a dc)*, dc in each rem ch across, ch 27, turn. *(31 dc)*

Row 2: Dc in 6th ch from hook *(beg 5 sk chs count as a dc and ch-1 sp)*, [ch 1, sk next ch, dc in next ch] 10 times, ch 1, sk next ch, *dc in next dc**, ch 1, sk next dc, rep from * across, ending last rep at **, turn. *(28 dc, 27 ch-1 sps)*

Row 3: Ch 3 *(see Pattern Notes)*, sk first st, dc in each ch-1 sp and in each dc across, turn. *(55 dc)*

Row 4: Ch 3, sk first st, dc in next 2 dc, *ch 1, sk next dc, dc in next 3 dc, rep from * across, turn. *(42 dc, 13 ch-1 sps)*

Row 5: Ch 3, sk first st, dc in each dc and in each ch-1 sp across, turn.

Row 6: Ch 4 *(see Pattern Notes)*, sk first 2 sts, *dc in next dc**, ch 1, sk next dc, rep from * across, ending last rep at **, turn.

Rows 7–34 [7–38, 7–42, 7–46, 7–50, 7–54, 7–58]: [Rep rows 3–6 consecutively] 7 [8, 9, 10, 11, 12, 13] times.

Body Back

Row 1: Ch 3, sk first st, [dc in next ch-1 sp, dc in next dc] 15 times, ch 26, turn. *(31 dc)*

Row 2: Dc in 4th ch from hook *(beg 3 sk chs count as a dc)*, dc in next ch, [ch 1, sk next ch, dc in each of next 3 chs] 5 times, ch 1, sk next ch, *dc in each of next 3 dc**, ch 1, sk next dc, rep from * across, ending last rep at **, turn.

Row 3: Ch 3, sk first st, dc in each dc and each ch-1 sp across, turn. *(57 dc)*

Row 4: Ch 4, sk first 2 sts, *dc in next dc**, ch 1, sk next dc, rep from * across, ending last rep at **, turn.

Row 5: Ch 3, sk first st, dc in each ch-1 sp and each dc across, turn.

Row 6: Ch 3, sk first st, dc in next 2 dc, *ch 1, sk next dc, dc in next 3 dc, rep from * across, turn.

Rows 7–34 [7–38, 7–42, 7–46, 7–50, 7–54, 7–58]: [Rep rows 3–6 consecutively] 7 [8, 9, 10, 11, 12, 13] times. Fasten off.

Sew first and last rows of Body tog.

Bodice

Rnd 1 (RS): Working in ends of rows on RS, **join** *(see Pattern Notes)* yarn in first row of Body, **ch 3** *(see Pattern Notes)*, dc in same row, *2 dc in each of next 5 [7, 7, 9, 7, 7, 9] rows, 3 dc in each of next 5 [5, 5, 5, 9, 9, 9] rows, 2 dc in each of next 6 [6, 8, 8, 8, 10, 10] rows, 3 dc in next row, 2 dc in each of next 6 [6, 8, 8, 8, 10, 10] rows, 3 dc in each of next 5 [5, 5, 5, 9, 9, 9] rows, 2 dc in each of next 5 [7, 7, 9, 7, 7, 9] rows**, 3 dc in next row, rep from * once, ending last rep at **, dc in first row, join in 3rd ch of beg ch-3, turn. *(160 [176, 192, 208, 240, 256, 272] dc)*

Sizes Small, Large & 3X-Large Only

Rnd 2: Ch 3, sk first st, dc in each of next 3 dc, *ch 1, sk next dc**, dc in each of next 7 sts, rep from * around, ending last rep at **, dc in each of next 3 dc, join, turn. *(140 [168, 224] dc, 20 [24, 32] ch sps)*

Rnd 3: Ch 3, sk first st, dc in next dc, *[ch 1, sk next dc, dc in each of next 7 sts] 4 [5, 7] times, ch 1 sk next dc**, dc in each of next 11 sts, [ch 1, sk next dc, dc in each of next 7 sts] 4 [5, 7] times, ch 1 sk next dc, dc in each of next 3 sts, rep from * around, ending last rep at **, dc in next dc, join in 3rd ch of beg ch-3, sl st in next dc, turn. *(140 [168, 224] dc, 20 [24, 32] ch sps)*

Rnd 4: Ch 4 *(see Pattern Notes)*, sk first 2 sts, *dc in each of next 7 sts, ch 1, sk next dc, rep from * around to last 6 sts, dc in each of last 6 sts, join in 3rd ch of beg ch-4, sl st in next ch-1 sp, turn.

Rnd 5: Ch 3, sk first st, dc in each of next 5 dc, *[ch 1, sk next dc, dc in each of next 7 sts] 4 [5, 7] times, ch 1, sk next dc**, dc in each of next 3 sts, rep from * to **, dc in each of next 11 sts, rep from * around, ending last rep at **, dc in next 5 dc, join in 3rd ch of beg ch-3, turn.

STITCH KEY
◯ Chain (ch)
• Slip stitch (sl st)
┬ Double crochet (dc)
⟶ Direction of work

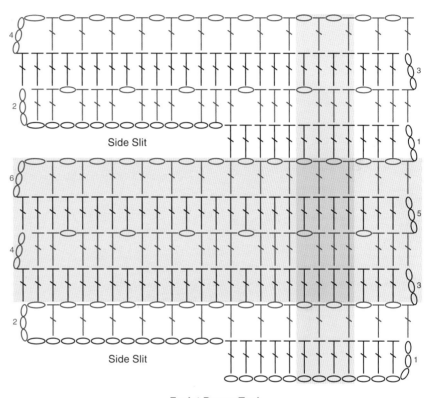

Eyelet Dream Tank
Reduced Sample of Body Stitch Diagram
Note: Reps shown in gray.

Center Stitch
of Front and Back

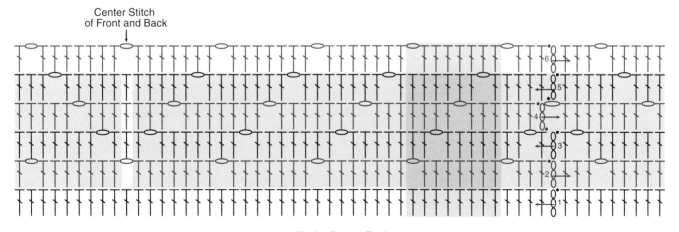

Eyelet Dream Tank
Reduced Sample of Bodice Stitch Diagram
Note: Reps shown in gray.

Rnds 6–9 [6–9, 6–13]: [Rep rnds 2–5] 1 [1, 2] time(s).

Rnd 10 [10, 14]: Rep rnd 2.

Sizes Medium, X-Large, 2X-Large & 4X-Large Only

Rnd [2]: Ch 3, sk first st, dc in each of next 3 dc, *ch 1, sk next dc**, dc in each of next 7 sts, rep from * around, ending last rep at **, dc in each of next 3 dc, join in 3rd ch of beg ch-3, turn. ([154, 182, 210, 238] dc, [22, 26, 30, 34] ch sps)

Rnd [3]: Ch 3, sk first st, dc in next dc, *[ch 1, sk next dc, dc in each of next 7 sts] 5 [6, 7, 8] times, ch 1, sk next dc**, dc in each of next 3 sts, rep from * around, ending last rep at **, dc in next dc, join in 3rd ch of beg ch-3, sl st in next dc, turn. ([152, 180, 208, 236] dc, [24, 28, 32, 36] ch sps)

Rnd [4]: Ch 4, sk first 2 sts, *dc in each of next 7 sts, ch 1, sk next dc, rep from * around, dc in next 6 sts, join in 3rd ch of beg ch-4, sl st in next ch-1 sp, turn.

Rnd [5]: Ch 3, sk first st, dc in next 5 dc, *[ch 1, sk next dc, dc in next 7 sts] 4 [5, 6, 7] times, ch 1 sk next dc**, dc in next 11 sts, rep from * around, ending last rep at **, dc in each of in next 5 sts, join in 3rd ch of beg ch-3, turn.

Rnds [6–9]: Rep rnds 2–5.

Rnds [10–12]: Rep rnds 2–4. At end of last rnd, do not sl st in next ch-1 sp, turn.

Shape Left Front Armhole

Row 1: Now working in rows, sl st in each of first 3 [6, 19, 22, 22, 35, 38] sts, ch 1, hdc in next ch-1 sp, dc in each of next 5 dc, *[ch 1, sk next dc, dc in each of next 7 sts] 3 [3, 3, 3, 4, 4, 4] times, ch 1, sk next dc*, dc in next 3 sts, **dc dec** (see Stitch Guide) in next 2 dc, turn. (30 [30, 30, 30, 37, 37, 37] dc, 1 hdc, 4 [4, 4, 4, 5, 5, 5] ch sps)

Row 2: Ch 2, sk first st, dc in next st, dc in each of next 4 sts, *ch 1, sk next dc, dc in each of next 7 sts, rep from * across to last 5 sts, ch 1, sk next dc, [dc dec in next 2 sts] twice, turn. (28 [28, 28, 28, 35, 35, 35] dc, 4 [4, 4, 4, 5, 5, 5] ch sps)

Row 3: Ch 2, sk first st, dc in next st, dc dec in next 2 sts, dc in each next 4 dc, [ch 1, sk next dc, dc in each of next 7 sts] 2 [2, 2, 2, 3, 3, 3] times, ch 1, sk next dc, dc in each of next 3 sts, [dc dec in next 2 sts] 2 times, turn. (25 [25, 25, 25, 32, 32, 32] dc, 3 [3, 3, 3, 4, 4, 4] ch sps)

Sizes 2X-Large, 3X-Large & 4X-Large Only

Row [4]: Ch 2, sk first st, dc in next dc, dc dec in next 2 sts, dc in each of next 3 sts, *ch 1, sk next dc, dc in each of next 7 sts, rep from * until 5 sts rem, ch 1, sk next dc, dc in each of next 4 sts, turn. ([30] dc, [4] ch sps)

Row [5]: Ch 3, sk first st, dc in next dc, [ch 1, sk next dc, dc in each of next 7 sts] 3 times, ch 1, sk next dc, dc in each of next 3 sts, [dc dec in next 2 sts] 2 times, turn. ([28] dc, [4] ch sps)

Row [6]: Ch 2, sk first st, dc in next st, dc dec in next 2 sts, dc in each of next 3 sts, *ch 1, sk next dc, dc in each of next 7 sts, rep from * across to last dc, dc in last dc, turn. ([27] dc, [3] ch sps)

Row [7]: Ch 3, dc in each of next 5 dc, [ch 1, sk next dc, dc in each of next 7 sts] 2 times, ch 1, sk next dc, dc in each of next 3 sts, [dc dec in next 2 sts] 2 times, turn. ([25] dc, [3] ch sps)

Shape V-Neck

Row 1: Ch 2, sk first st, dc in next dc, dc dec in next 2 sts, dc in each of next 3 sts, *ch 1, sk next dc, dc in each of next 7 sts, rep from * across to last 5 sts, ch 1, sk next dc, dc in last 4 sts, turn. (23 dc, 3 ch sps)

Row 2: Ch 3, sk first st, dc in next dc, [ch 1, sk next dc, dc in each of next 7 sts] twice, ch 1, sk next dc, dc in each of next 3 sts, [dc dec in next 2 sts] twice, turn. (21 dc, 3 ch sps)

Row 3: Ch 2, sk first st, dc in next st, dc dec in next 2 sts, dc each of in next 3 sts, *ch 1, sk next dc, dc in each of next 7 sts, rep from * across to last dc, dc in last dc, turn. *(20 dc, 2 ch sps)*

Row 4: Ch 3, sk first st, dc in each of next 5 sts, ch 1, sk next dc, dc in each of next 7 sts, ch 1, sk next dc, dc in each of next 3 dc, [dc dec in next 2 sts] twice, turn. *(18 dc, 2 ch sps)*

Row 5: Ch 2, sk first st, dc in next st, dc dec in next 2 sts, dc in each of next 3 sts, ch 1, sk next dc, dc in each of next 7 sts, ch 1, sk next dc, dc in each of next 4 sts, turn. *(16 dc, 2 ch sps)*

Row 6: Ch 3, sk first st, dc in next dc, *ch 1, sk next dc, dc in each of next 7 sts, rep from * across, turn.

Row 7: Ch 3, sk first st, dc in next st, *ch 1, sk next dc, dc in each of next 7 sts, rep from * across, dc in next dc, turn.

Row 8: Ch 3, sk first st, dc in next 5 dc, ch 1, sk next dc, dc in each of next 7 sts, ch 1, sk next dc, dc in each of next 3 sts, turn.

Row 9: Ch 3, sk first st, dc in each of next 4 dc, *ch 1, sk next dc, dc in each of next 7 sts, ch 1, sk next dc, dc in each of next 4 sts, turn.

Sizes Large & X-Large Only
Rows [10–13]: Rep rows 6–9.

All Sizes
Rows 10–12 [10–12, 14–16, 14–16, 10–12, 10–12, 10–12]: Rep rows 6–8.

Row 13 [13, 17, 17, 13, 13, 13]: Ch 3, 3 dc in first dc, *ch 1, sk next dc, dc in each of next 7 sts, rep from * across to last dc, dc in last dc, turn. *(19 dc, 2 ch sps)*

Row 14 [14, 18, 18, 14, 14, 14]: Ch 3, sk first st, dc in next dc, [ch 1, sk next dc, dc in each of next 7 sts] 2 times, ch 1, sk next dc, dc in next dc, 2 dc in next dc. Fasten off. *(19 dc, 3 ch sps)*

Shape Right Front Armhole
Row 1: Hold Bodice with RS facing, sk 1 dc from Left Front, join yarn in next dc, ch 2, dc in each of next 4 sts, [ch 1, sk next dc, dc in each of next 7 sts] 3 [3, 3, 3, 4, 4, 4] times, ch 1, sk next dc, dc in each of next 5 sts, **sc dec** *(see Stitch Guide)* in next ch-1 sp and next dc, turn. *(30 [30, 30, 30, 37, 37, 37] dc, 1 sc, 4 [4, 4, 4, 5, 5, 5] ch sps)*

Row 2: Ch 2, sk first st, dc in next st, dc dec in next 2 dc, [ch 1, sk next dc, dc in each of next 7 sts] 3 times, ch 1, sk next dc, dc in each of next 4 sts, dc dec in next 2 sts, turn. *(28 [28, 28, 28, 35, 35, 35] dc, 4 [4, 4, 4, 5, 5, 5] ch sps)*

Row 3: Ch 2, sk first st, dc in next st, dc dec in next 2 dc, dc in each of next 3 dc, [ch 1, sk next dc, dc in each of next 7 sts] 2 [2, 2, 2, 3, 3, 3] times, ch 1, sk next dc, dc in each of next 4 sts, [dc dec in next 2 sts] twice, turn. *(25 [25, 25, 25, 32, 32, 32] dc, 3 [3, 3, 3, 4, 4, 4] ch sps)*

Sizes 2X-Large, 3X-Large & 4X-Large Only
Row [4]: Ch 3, dc in next 3 sts, [ch 1, sk next dc, dc in each of next 7 sts] 3 times, ch 1, sk next dc, dc in each of next 3 sts, [dc dec in next 2 sts] twice, turn. *([30] dc, [4] ch sps)*

Row [5]: Ch 2, dc in next st, dc dec in next 2 dc, dc in each of next 3 sts, *ch 1, sk next dc, dc in each of next 7 sts, rep from * across to last 3 dc, ch 1, sk next dc, dc in last 2 dc, turn. *([28] dc, [4] ch sps)*

Row [6]: Ch 3, [dc in each of next 7 sts, sk next dc, ch 1] 3 times, dc in each of next 3 sts, [dc dec in next 2 sts] twice, turn. *([27] dc, [3] ch sps)*

Row [7]: Ch 2, dc in next st, dc dec in next 2 sts, dc in each of next 3 sts, [ch 1, sk next dc, dc in each of next 7 sts] twice, ch 1, sk next dc, dc in each of next 6 sts, turn. *([25] dc, [3] ch sps)*

Shape V-Neck

Row 1: Ch 3, sk first st, dc in each of next 3 dc, [ch 1, sk next dc, dc in each of next 7 sts] twice, ch 1, sk next dc, dc in each of next 3 sts, [dc dec in next 2 sts] twice, turn. *(23 dc, 3 ch sps)*

Row 2: Ch 2, sk first st, dc in next dc, dc dec in next 2 sts, dc in each of next 3 sts, [ch 1, sk next dc, dc in each of next 7 sts] twice, ch 1, sk next dc, dc in next 2 dc, turn. *(21 dc, 3 ch sps)*

Row 3: Ch 3, sk first st, [dc in each of next 7 sts, ch 1, sk next dc] 2 times, dc in each of next 3 sts, [dc dec in next 2 sts] twice, turn. *(20 dc, 2 ch sps)*

Row 4: Ch 2, sk first st, dc in next dc, dc dec in next 2 sts, dc each of in next 3 dc, ch 1, sk next dc, dc in each of next 7 sts, ch 1, sk next dc, dc in each of next 6 dc, turn. *(18 dc, 2 ch sps)*

Row 5: Ch 3, sk first st, dc in each of next 3 sts, ch 1, sk next dc, dc in each of next 7 sts, ch 1, sk next dc, dc in each of next 3 sts, [dc dec in next 2 sts] 2 times, turn. *(16 dc, 2 ch sps)*

Row 6: Ch 3, sk first st, dc in each of next 6 sts, ch 1, sk next dc, dc in each of next 7 sts, ch 1, sk next dc, dc in each of next 2 sts, turn.

Row 7: Ch 3, sk first st, [dc in each of next 7 sts, ch 1, sk next dc] 2 times, dc in next dc, turn.

Row 8: Ch 3, sk first st, dc in each of next 2 sts, ch 1, sk next dc, dc in each of next 7 sts, ch 1, sk next dc, dc in each of next 6 sts, turn.

Row 9: Ch 3, sk first st, dc in each of next 3 dc, ch 1, sk next dc, dc in each of next 7 sts, ch 1, sk next dc, dc in each of next 5 sts, turn.

Sizes Large & X-Large Only

Rows [10–13]: Rep rows 6–9.

All Sizes

Rows 10–12 [10–12, 14–16, 14–16, 10–12, 10–12, 10–12]: Rep rows 6–8.

Row 13 [13, 17, 17, 13, 13, 13]: Ch 3, sk first st, [dc in each of next 7 dc, ch 1, sk next dc] 2 times, ch 1, sk next dc, 4 dc in next dc, turn. *(19 dc, 2 ch sps)*

Row 14 [14, 18, 18, 14, 14, 14]: Ch 3, dc in first st, dc in next dc, [ch 1, sk next dc, dc in each of next 7 sts] 2 times, ch 1, sk next dc, dc in each of next 2 sts. Fasten off. *(19 dc, 3 ch sps)*

Back Armhole Shaping

Row 1: Hold Bodice with RS facing, sk 5 [13, 21, 29, 29, 37, 45] sts from Right Front, join yarn in next dc, ch 1, hdc in next ch-1 sp, dc in each of next 5 dc, *[ch 1, sk next dc, dc in each of next 7 sts] 3 [3, 3, 3, 4, 4, 4] times, ch 1, sk next dc*, dc in each of next 11 sts, rep from * to *, dc in each of next 5 dc, sc dec in next ch-1 sp and next dc, turn. *(63 [63, 63, 63, 77, 77, 77] dc, 1 hdc, 1 sc, 8 [8, 8, 8, 10, 10, 10] ch sps)*

Row 2: Ch 2, sk first st, dc in next st, dc dec in next 2 dc, *ch 1, sk next dc, dc in each of next 7 sts, rep from * across to last 5 sts, ch 1, sk next dc, [dc dec in next 2 sts] twice, turn. *(60 [60, 60, 60, 74, 74, 74] dc, 9 [9, 9, 9, 11, 11, 11] ch sps)*

Row 3: Ch 2, sk first st, dc in next st, dc dec in next 2 sts, dc in next 4 dc, *[ch 1, sk next dc, dc in each of next 7 sts] 3 times, ch 1, sk next dc**, dc in each of next 3 sts, rep from * across, ending last rep at **, dc in each of next 4 sts, [dc dec in next 2 sts] twice, turn. *(57 [57, 57, 57, 71, 71, 71] dc, 8 [8, 8, 8, 10, 10, 10] ch sps)*

Sizes 2X-Large, 3X-Large & 4X-Large Only

Row [4]: Ch 2, sk first st, dc in next st, dc dec in next 2 sts, *ch 1, sk next dc, dc in each of next 7 sts, rep from * across to last 5 sts, ch 1, sk next dc, [dc dec in next 2 sts] twice, turn. *([67] dc, [10] ch sps)*

Row [5]: Ch 2, sk first st, dc in next st, dc dec in next 2 sts, dc in each of next 4 dc, *[ch 1, sk next dc, dc in each of next 7 sts] 3 times*, ch 1, sk next dc, dc in each of next 11 sts, rep from * to *, ch 1, sk next dc, dc in each of next 4 dc, [dc dec in next 2 sts] twice. *([65] dc, [8] ch sps)*

Row [6]: Rep row 4. *([60] dc, [9] ch sps)*

Row [7]: Ch 2, sk first st, dc in next st, dc dec in next 2 sts, dc in each of next 4 dc, *[ch 1, sk next dc, dc in each of next 7 sts] 3 times*, ch 1, sk next dc, dc in each of next 3 sts, rep from * to *, ch 1, sk next dc, dc in each of next 4 dc, [dc dec in next 2 sts] twice. *([57] dc, [8] ch sps)*

Back

Row 1: Ch 3, sk first st, dc in each of next 3 dc, *ch 1, sk next dc, dc in each of next 7 sts, rep from * across to last 5 sts, ch 1, sk next dc, dc in each of last 4 sts, turn. *(57 dc, 8 ch sps)*

Row 2: Ch 3, sk first st, dc in next dc, *[ch 1, sk next dc, dc in each of next 7 sts] 3 times, ch 1, sk next dc**, dc in each of next 11 sts, rep from * across, ending last rep at **, dc in each of next 2 sts, turn. *(57 dc, 8 ch sps)*

Row 3: Ch 3, sk first st, *dc in each of next 7 sts**, ch 1, sk next dc, rep from * across, ending last rep at **, dc in next dc, turn. *(58 dc, 7 ch sps)*

Row 4: Ch 3, sk first st, dc in each of next 5 sts, *[ch 1, sk next dc, dc in each of next 7 sts], 3 times, ch 1, sk next dc*, dc in each of next 3 dc, rep from * to *, dc in each of next 6 dc, turn. *(57 dc, 8 ch sps)*

Sizes Small, Medium, Large, X-Large & 4X-Large Only

Rows 5–8: Rep rows 1–4.

All sizes

Row 9 [9, 9, 9, 5, 5, 9]: Rep row 1. Fasten off.

Assembly

Sew shoulder seams.

Neck Edging

With RS facing and working in ends of rows, sts and ch sps, join yarn in left shoulder seam, sc evenly sp around, join in beg sc. Fasten off.

Armhole Edging

With RS facing and working in ends of rows, sts and ch sps, join yarn at bottom of 1 Armhole, sc evenly sp around, join in beg sc. Fasten off.

Rep for rem Armhole.

Bottom Edging

With RS facing and working in ends of rows, sts and ch sps, join yarn at top of left hemline slit, sc evenly sp around, join in beg sc. Fasten off. ●

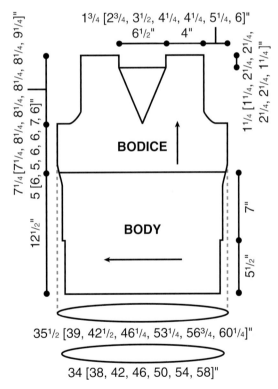

Note: Arrow indicates direction of work.

Timeless Grace Tank

Skill Level

 INTERMEDIATE

Finished Sizes

Instructions given fit size small; changes for medium, large, X-large, 2X-large, 3X-large and 4X-large are in [ ].

Finished Measurement

Bust: 35½ inches *(small)* [40 inches *(medium)*, 44½ inches *(large)*, 48 inches *(X-large)*, 51½ inches *(2X-large)*, 56 inches *(3X-large)*, 60½ inches *(4X-large)*]

Materials

- Omega Eulali super fine (fingering) weight cotton yarn (3½ oz/394 yds/100g per skein):
  3 [3, 4, 4, 4, 5, 5] skeins #18 cream
- Size 7/4.5mm crochet hook or size needed to obtain gauge
- Tapestry needle

Gauge

21 sts and 16 pattern rows = 4 inches

Pattern Notes

Weave in loose ends as work progresses.

Join with slip stitch as indicated unless otherwise stated.

Joining half double crochet counts as a chain space.

Special Stitches

First foundation single crochet (first foundation sc): Ch 2, insert hook into 2nd ch from hook, yo, pull up lp, yo, pull through 1 lp on hook *(ch-1 completed)*, yo, pull through 1 lp on hook *(sc completed)*.

Next foundation single crochet (next foundation sc): Insert hook in last ch-1 made, yo, pull up lp, yo, pull through 1 lp on hook *(ch-1)*, yo, pull through all lps on hook *(sc)* as indicated.

Tank

Body

Rnd 1: First foundation sc *(see Special Stitches)*, 185 [209, 233, 251, 269, 293, 317] **next foundation sc** *(see Special Stitches)*, **join** *(see Pattern Notes)* in first foundation sc, turn. *(186 [210, 234, 252, 270, 294, 318] sc)*

Rnd 2 (RS): Ch 1, sc in first sc, ch 2, *[sk next 2 sc, 3 sc in next sc] 7 [8, 8, 8, 9, 9, 9] times, **ch 2, sk next 2 sc, sc in next sc, ch 2, [sk next 2 sc, 3 sc in next sc] 4 [4, 5, 5, 5, 5, 5] times, rep from ** once, ch 2, sk next 2 sc, sc in next sc, ch 2, [sk next 2 sc, 3 sc in next sc] 7 [8, 8, 8, 9, 9, 9] times, ch 2, sk next 2 sc, sc in next sc, ch 2, [sk next 2 sc, 3 sc in next sc] 4 [6, 8, 11, 12, 16, 20] times***, ch 2, sk next 2 sc, sc in next sc, ch 2, rep from * once, ending rep at ***, sk next 2 sc, **join with hdc in first sc** *(see Pattern Notes)*, turn. *(166 [190, 214, 232, 250, 274, 298] sc, 20 ch sps)*

Rnd 3: Ch 1, sc in joining hdc, sk next sc, *[3 sc in next sc, sk next 2 sc] 3 [5, 7, 9, 11, 15, 19] times, 3 sc in next sc, sk next sc, sc in next ch, ch 3, sk next 3 sts, sc in next ch, sk next sc, [3 sc in next sc, sk next 2 sc] 6 [7, 7, 7, 8, 8, 8] times, **3 sc in next sc, sk next sc, sc in next ch, ch 3, sk next 3 sts, sc in next ch, sk next sc, {3 sc in next sc, sk next 2 sc} 3 [3, 4, 4, 4, 4, 4] times, rep from ** once, 3 sc in next sc, sk next sc, sc in next ch, ch 3, sk next 3 sts, sc in next ch, sk next sc, [3 sc in next sc, sk next 2 sc] 6 [7, 7, 7, 8, 8, 8] times, 3 sc in

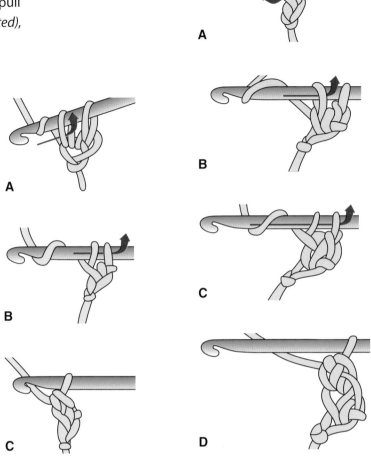

First Foundation Single Crochet   **Next Foundation Single Crochet**

next sc, sk next sc***, sc in next ch, rep from * once, ending rep at ***, join with hdc in first sc, turn. *(176 [200, 224, 242, 260, 284, 308] sc, 10 ch sps)*

Rnd 4: Ch 1, sc in joining hdc, ch 2, *[sk next 2 sc, 3 sc in next sc] 7 [8, 8, 8, 9, 9, 9] times, **ch 2, sk next 3 sts, sc in next ch, ch 2, sk next ch, { sk next 2 sc, 3 sc in next sc } 4 [4, 5, 5, 5, 5, 5] times, rep from ** once, ch 2, sk next 3 sts, sc in next ch, ch 2, sk next ch, [sk next 2 sc, 3 sc in next sc] 7 [8, 8, 8, 9, 9, 9] times, ch 2, sk next 3 sts, sc in next ch, ch 2, sk next ch, [sk next 2 sc, 3 sc in next sc] 4 [6, 8, 11, 12, 16, 20] times***, ch 2, sk next 3 sts, sc in next ch, ch 2, sk next ch, rep from * once, ending rep at ***, sk next 2 sc, join with hdc in first sc, turn.

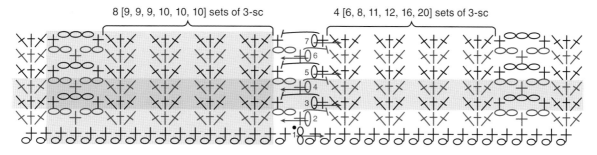

8 [9, 9, 9, 10, 10, 10] sets of 3-sc   4 [6, 8, 11, 12, 16, 20] sets of 3-sc

Timeless Grace Tank
Reduced Sample of Stitch Diagram
Note: *Reps shown in gray.*

STITCH KEY

○ Chain (ch)

• Slip stitch (sl st)

+ Single crochet (sc)

T Half double crochet (hdc)

First foundation single crochet (first foundation sc)

Next foundation single crochet (next foundation sc)

→ Direction of work

Rnds 5–68: [Rep rnds 3 and 4] 32 times.

Rnd 69: Ch 1, sc in joining hdc, sk next sc, [3 sc in next sc, sk next 2 sc] 3 [5, 7, 9, 11, 15, 19] times, 3 sc in next sc, sk next sc, sc in next ch, ch 3, sk next 3 sts, sc in next ch, sk next sc, [3 sc in next sc, sk next 2 sc] 6 [7, 7, 7, 8, 8, 8] times, *[3 sc in next sc, sk next sc, sc in next ch, ch 3, sk next 3 sts, sc in next ch, sk next sc, {3 sc in next sc, sk next 2 sc} 3 [3, 4, 4, 4, 4, 4] times, rep from * once, 3 sc in next sc, sk next sc, sc in next ch, ch 3, sk next 3 sts, sc in next ch, sk next sc, [3 sc in next sc, sk next 2 sc] 6 [7, 7, 7, 8, 8, 8] times, 3 sc in next sc, sk next sc, sc in next ch, ch 3, sk next 3 sts, sc in next ch, sk next sc, 3 sc in next sc, sk next sc, sc in next ch, ch 3, sk next 2 sts, sl st in next sc, sl st in each of next 5 [5, 5, 11, 11, 11, 11] sc, turn.

Back Armhole Shaping

Row 1: Now working in rows, ch 1, sc in first sc, [sk next 2 sc, 3 sc in next sc] 1 [1, 1, 3, 3, 3, 3] time(s), ch 2, sk next 3 sts, sc in next ch, ch 2, sk next ch, [sk next 2 sc, 3 sc in next sc] 7 [8, 8, 8, 9, 9, 9] times, *ch 2, sk next 3 sts, sc in next ch, ch 2, sk next ch, [sk next 2 sc, 3 sc in next sc] 4 [4, 5, 5, 5, 5, 5] times, rep from * once, ch 2, sk next 3 sts, sc in next ch, ch 2, sk next ch, [sk next 2 sc, 3 sc in next sc] 7 [8, 8, 8, 9, 9, 9] times, ch 2, sk next 3 sts, sc in next ch, ch 2, sk next ch, [sk next 2 sc, 3 sc in next sc] 1 [1, 1, 3, 3, 3, 3] time(s), sk next 2 sc, sc in next sc, turn. *(79 [85, 91, 103, 109, 109, 109] sc, 10 ch sps)*

Sizes X-Large, 2X-Large, 3X-Large & 4X-Large Only

Row [2]: Ch 1, [sk next 2 sc, 3 sc in next sc] 3 times, sk next sc, sc in next ch, ch 3, sk next 3 sts, sc in next ch, sk next sc, [3 sc in next sc, sk next 2 sc] [7, 8, 8, 8] times, 3 sc in next sc, *[sk next sc, sc in next ch, ch 3, sk next 3 sts, sc in next ch, sk next sc, {3 sc in next sc, sk next 2 sc} 4 times, 3 sc in next sc] twice, rep from * once, sk next sc, sc in next ch, ch 3, sk next 3 sts, sc in next ch, sk next sc, [3 sc in next sc, sk next 2 sc] twice, 2 sc in next sc, **sc dec** *(see Stitch Guide)* in same and last sc, turn. *([106, 112, 112, 112] sc, [5] ch sps)*

Row [3]: Ch 1, sk first sc, sc in next sc, [sk next 2 sc, 3 sc in next sc] twice, ch 2, sk next 3 sts, sc in next ch, ch 2, sk next ch, [sk next 2 sc, 3 sc in next sc] [8, 9, 9, 9] times, [ch 2, sk next 3 sts, sc in next ch, ch 2, sk next ch, {sk next 2 sc, 3 sc in next sc} 5 times] twice, ch 2, sk next 3 sts, sc in next ch, ch 2, sk next ch, [sk next 2 sc, 3 sc in next sc] [8, 9, 9, 9] times, ch 2, sk next 3 sts, sc in next ch, ch 2, sk next ch, [sk next 2 sc, 3 sc in next sc] twice, sk next 2 sc, sc in next sc, turn. *([97, 103, 103, 103] sc, [10] ch sps)*

Row [4]: Ch 1, [sk next 2 sc, 3 sc in next sc] 2 times, sk next sc, sc in next ch, ch 3, sk next 3 sts, sc in next ch, sk next sc, [3 sc in next sc, sk next 2 sc] [7, 8, 8, 8] times, 3 sc in next sc, [sk next sc, sc in next ch, ch 3, sk next 3 sts, sc in next ch, sk next sc, {3 sc in next sc, sk next 2 sc} 4 times, 3 sc in next sc] twice, sk next sc, sc in next ch, ch 3, sk next 3 sts, sc in next ch, sk next sc, [3 sc in next sc, sk next 2 sc] [7, 8, 8, 8] times, 3 sc in next sc, sk next sc, sc in next ch, ch 3, sk next 3 sts, sc in next ch, sk next sc, 3 sc in next sc, sk next 2 sc, 2 sc in next sc, sc dec in same and last sc, turn. ([100, 106, 106, 106] sc, [5] ch sps)

Row [5]: Ch 1, sk first sc, sc in next sc, sk next 2 sc, 3 sc in next sc, ch 2, sk next 3 sts, sc in next ch, ch 2, sk next ch, [sk next 2 sc, 3 sc in next sc] [8, 9, 9, 9] times, [ch 2, sk next 3 sts, sc in next ch, ch 2, sk next ch, {sk next 2 sc, 3 sc in next sc} 5 times] twice, ch 2, sk next 3 sts, sc in next ch, ch 2, sk next ch, [sk next 2 sc, 3 sc in next sc] [8, 9, 9, 9] times, ch 2, sk next 3 sts, sc in next ch, ch 2, sk next ch, sk next 2 sc, 3 sc in next sc, sk next 2 sc, sc in next sc, turn. ([91, 97, 97, 97] sc, [10] ch sps)

All Sizes

Row 2 [2, 2, 6, 6, 6, 6]: Ch 1, sk first 2 sc, 3 sc in next sc, sk next sc, sc in next ch, ch 3, sk next 3 sts, sc in next ch, sk next sc, [3 sc in next sc, sk next 2 sc] 6 [7, 7, 7, 8, 8, 8] times, 3 sc in next sc, [sk next sc, sc in next ch, ch 3, sk next 3 sts, sc in next ch, sk next sc, {3 sc in next sc, sk next 2 sc } 3 [3, 4, 4, 4, 4, 4] times, 3 sc in next sc] twice, sk next sc, sc in next ch, ch 3, sk next 3 sts, sc in next ch, sk next sc, [3 sc in next sc, sk next 2 sc] 6 [7, 7, 7, 8, 8, 8] times, 3 sc in next sc, sk next sc, sc in next ch, ch 3, sk next 3 sts, sc in next ch, sk next sc, 2 sc in next sc, sc dec in same sc and last sc, turn. (82 [88, 94, 94, 100, 100, 100] sc, 5 ch sps)

Row 3 [3, 3, 7, 7, 7, 7]: Ch 1, sk first sc, sc in next sc, ch 2, sk next 3 sts, sc in next ch, ch 2, sk next ch, [sk next 2 sc, 3 sc in next sc] 7 [8, 8, 8, 9, 9, 9] times, [ch 2, sk next 3 sts, sc in next ch, ch 2, sk next ch, {sk next 2 sc, 3 sc in next sc } 4 [4, 5, 5, 5, 5, 5] times] twice, ch 2, sk next 3 sts, sc in next ch, ch 2, sk next ch, [sk next 2 sc, 3 sc in next sc] 7 [8, 8, 8, 9, 9, 9] times, ch 2, sk next 3 sts, sc in next ch, ch 2, sk next ch, sk next 2 sc, sc in next sc, turn. (73 [79, 85, 85, 91, 91 91] sc, 10 ch sps)

Row 4 [4, 4, 8, 8, 8, 8]: Ch 3, sk first 5 sts, sc in next ch, sk next sc, [3 sc in next sc, sk next 2 sts] 6 [7, 7, 7, 8, 8, 8] times, 3 sc in next sc, [sk next sc, sc in next ch, ch 3, sk next 3 sts, sc in next ch, sk next sc, {3 sc in next sc, sk next 2 sts} 3 [3, 4, 4, 4, 4, 4] times, 3 sc in next sc] twice, sk next sc, sc in next ch, ch 3, sk next 3 sts, sc in next ch, sk next sc, sk next sc, sc in next ch, ch 3, sk next 3 sts, sc in next ch, sk next sc, [3 sc in next sc, sk next 2 sts] 6 [7, 7, 7, 8, 8, 8] times, 3 sc in next sc, sk next sc, sc in next ch, sk next 4 sts, dc in last sc, turn. (74 [80, 86, 86, 92, 92, 92] sc, 5 ch sps)

Row 5 [5, 5, 9, 9, 9, 9]: Ch 1, sk first 3 sts, [3 sc in next sc, sk next 2 sts] 7 [8, 8, 8, 9, 9, 9] times, *ch 2, sk next ch, sc in next ch, ch 2, sk next 3 sts, {3 sc in next sc, sk next 2 sts} 4 [4, 5, 5, 5, 5, 5] times, rep from * once, ch 2, sk next ch, sc in next ch, ch 2, sk next 3 sts, [3 sc in next sc, sk next 2 sts] 6 [7, 7, 7, 8, 8, 8] times, 2 sc in next sc, sc dec in same sc and last sc, turn. (69 [75, 81, 81, 87, 87, 87] sc, 6 ch sps)

Back

Row 1: Ch 1, sk first sc, [3 sc in next sc, sk next 2 sts] 6 [7, 7, 7, 8, 8, 8] times, 3 sc in next sc, [sk next sc, sc in next ch, ch 3, sk next 3 sts, sc in next ch, sk next sc, {3 sc in next sc, sk next 2 sts} 3 [3, 4, 4, 4, 4, 4] times, 3 sc in next sc] twice, sk next sc, sc in next ch, ch 3, sk next 3 sts, sc in next ch, sk next sc, [3 sc in next sc, sk next 2 sts] 6 [7, 7, 7, 8, 8, 8] times, 3 sc in next sc, sk last sc, turn. (72 [78, 84, 84, 84, 90, 90, 90] sc, 3 ch sps)

Row 2: Ch 1, sk first sc, 3 sc in next sc, sk next 2 sts] 7 [8, 8, 8, 9, 9, 9] times, [ch 2, sk next ch, sc in next ch, ch 2, sk next 3 sts, {3 sc in next sc, sk next 2 sts} 4 [4, 5, 5, 5, 5, 5] times] twice, ch 2, sk next ch, sc in next ch, ch 2, sk next 3 sts, 3 sc in next sc, sk last sc, turn. *(69 [75, 81, 81, 87, 87, 87] sc, 6 ch sps)*

Rows 3–18 [3–20, 3–22, 3–18, 3–20, 3–20, 3–22]: [Rep rows 1 and 2] 8 [9, 10, 8, 9, 9, 10] times.

Left Shoulder

Row 1: Ch 1, sk first sc, [3 sc in next sc, sk next 2 sc] 6 [7, 7, 7, 8, 8, 8] times, 3 sc in next sc, sk next sc, sc in next ch, sk next 3 sts, dc in next ch, turn. *(22 [25, 25, 25, 28, 28, 28] sc, 1 dc)*

Row 2: Ch 1, sk first 3 sts, *3 sc in next sc**, sk next 2 sc, rep from * across, ending last rep at **, sk last sc, turn. *(21 [24, 24, 24, 27, 27, 27] sc)*

Row 3: Ch 1, sk first sc, *3 sc in next sc**, sk next 2 sc, rep from * across, ending last rep at **, sk last sc, turn.

Rows 4–7: Rep row 3. At end of last row, fasten off.

Right Shoulder

Row 1: With WS facing, sk next 29 [29, 35, 35, 35, 35, 35] sts from Left Shoulder, join in next ch, ch 3, sk next 3 sts, sc in next ch, sk next sc, *3 sc in next sc**, sk next 2 sc, rep from * across, ending last rep at **, sk last sc, turn. *(22 [25, 25, 25, 28, 28, 28] sc)*

Row 2: Ch 1, sk first sc, *3 sc in next sc, sk next 2 sc, rep from * across, sc in next ch, ch 1, turn.

Row 3: Ch 1, *sk next 2 sc, 3 sc in next sc, rep from * across, sk last sc, turn. *(21 [24, 24, 24, 27, 27, 27] sc)*

Row 4: Ch 1, sk first sc, *3 sc in next sc**, sk next 2 sc, rep from * across, ending last rep at **, sk last sc, turn.

Rows 5–7: Rep row 4. At end of last row, fasten off.

Front Armhole Shaping

Sk next 2 [8, 14, 11, 14, 26, 38] sts from last st of Back, join in next sc. Work same as Back Armhole Shaping.

Front

Row 1: Ch 1, sk first sc, [3 sc in next sc, sk next 2 sts] 6 [7, 7, 7, 8, 8, 8] times, 3 sc in next sc, *sk next sc, sc in next ch, ch 3, sk next 3 sts, sc in next ch, sk next sc, {3 sc in next sc, sk next 2 sts} 3 [3, 4, 4, 4, 4, 4] times, 3 sc in next sc, rep from * once, sk next sc, sc in next ch, ch 3, sk next 3 sts, sc in next ch, sk next sc, [3 sc in next sc, sk next 2 sts] 6 [7, 7, 7, 8, 8, 8] times, 3 sc in next sc, sk last sc, turn. *(72 [78, 84, 84, 90, 90, 90] sc, 3 ch sps)*

Row 2: Ch 1, sk first sc, [3 sc in next sc, sk next 2 sts] 7 [8, 8, 8, 9, 9, 9] times, [ch 2, sk next ch, sc in next ch, ch 2, sk next 3 sts, {3 sc in next sc, sk next 2 sts} 4 [4, 5, 5, 5, 5, 5] times] twice, ch 2, sk next ch, sc in next ch, ch 2, sk next 3 sts, 3 sc in next sc, sk next 2 sts, sk last sc, turn. *(69 [75, 81, 81, 87, 87, 87] sc, 6 ch sps)*

Rows 3–14 [3–16, 3–18, 3–12, 3–14, 3–14, 3–16]: [Rep rows 1 and 2] 8 [9, 10, 8, 9, 9, 10] times.

Right Shoulder

Row 1: Ch 1, sk first sc, [3 sc in next sc, sk next 2 sc] 6 [7, 7, 7, 8, 8, 8] times, 3 sc in next sc, sk next sc, sc in next ch, sk next 3 sts, dc in next ch, turn. *(22 [25, 25, 25, 28, 28, 28] sc, 1 dc)*

Row 2: Ch 1, sk first 3 sts, *3 sc in next sc**, sk next 2 sc, rep from * across, ending last rep at **, sk last sc, turn. *(21 [24, 24, 24, 27, 27, 27] sc)*

Row 3: Ch 1, sk first sc, *3 sc in next sc**, sk next 2 sc, rep from * across, ending last rep at **, sk last sc, turn.

Rows 4–10 [4–10, 4–10, 4–12, 4–12, 4–12, 4–12]: [Rep row 3] 7 [7, 7, 9, 9, 9, 9] times.

Row 11 [11, 11, 13, 13, 13, 13]: With RS tog, sl st in first sc of corresponding Back Shoulder, sk first sc on Front, sc in next sc, ch 1, sl st in next sc on Back, *sc in same sc on Front, ch 1, sl st in same sc on Back, sc in same sc on Front**, sk next 2 sc, sc in next sc, ch 1, sk next 2 sc on Back, sl st in next sc, rep from * across, ending last rep at **, sl st in last sc on Back. Fasten off.

Left Shoulder

Row 1: With WS facing, sk next 29 [29, 35, 35, 35, 35, 35] sts from Right Shoulder, join in next ch, ch 3, sk next 3 sts, sc in next ch, sk next sc, *3 sc in next sc**, sk next 2 sc, rep from * across, ending last rep at **, sk last sc, turn. *(22 [25, 25, 25, 28, 28, 28] sc)*

Row 2: Ch 1, sk first sc, *3 sc in next sc, sk next 2 sc, rep from * across, sc in next ch, turn.

Row 3: Ch 1, *sk next 2 sc, 3 sc in next sc, rep from * across, sk last sc, turn. *(21 [24, 24, 24, 27, 27, 27] sc)*

Row 4: Ch 1, sk first sc, *3 sc in next sc**, sk next 2 sc, rep from * across, ending last rep at **, sk last sc, ch 1, turn.

Rows 5–10 [5–10, 5–10, 5–12, 5–12, 5–12, 5–12]: [Rep row 4] 6 [6, 6, 8, 8, 8, 8] times. Fasten off.

Row 11 [11, 11, 13, 13, 13, 13]: With RS tog, sl st in first sc on corresponding back shoulder, sk first sc on Front, sc in next sc, ch 1, sl st in next sc on Back, *sc in same sc on Front, ch 1, sl st in same sc on Back, sc in same sc on front**, sk next 2 sc, sc in next sc, ch 1, sk next 2 sc on Back, sl st in next sc, rep from * across, ending last rep at **, sl st in last sc on Back. Fasten off.

Neck Edging

Hold piece with WS facing, working in sts and in ends of rows around neckline, join in center sc of first 3-sc group, ch 1, 3 sc in same sc as beg ch-1, [sk next 2 sts, 3 sc in next sc] 3 [3, 4, 4, 4, 4, 4] times, [3 sc in each of next 2 ch sps, [sk next 2 sts, 3 sc in next sc] 4 [4, 5, 5, 5, 5, 5] times, 3 sc in next row, [sk next row, 3 sc in next row] 8 [8, 8, 10, 10, 10, 10] times, 3 [3, 3, 0, 0, 0, 0] sc in next row, *sk next 2 sts, 3 sc in next sc] 4 [4, 5, 5, 5, 5, 5] times, 3 sc in each of next 2 ch sps, [sk next 2 sts, 3 sc in next sc,] 4 [4, 5, 5, 5, 5, 5] times, 3 sc in each of next 2 [2, 2, 0, 0, 0, 0] rows, [sk next row, 3 sc in next row] 8 [8, 8, 10, 10, 10, 10] times, join in first sc. Fasten off. *(126 [126, 138, 150, 150, 150, 150] sc)*

Armhole Edging

Size Small Only

With RS facing and working in sts and in ends of rows around 1 Armhole, join at center of underarm, 3 sc in same st, [sk next row, 3 sc in next row] 30 times, join in first sc. Fasten off. Rep around rem Armhole. *(93 sc)*

Sizes Medium, Large, X-Large, 2X-Large, 3X-Large & 4X-Large Only

With RS facing and working in sts and in ends of rows around 1 Armhole, join in center sc of first 3-sc group at underarm, 3 sc in same sc, [sk next 2 sts, 3 sc in next sc] [2, 4, 3, 4, 8, 12] times, 3 sc in next row, [sk next row, 3 sc in next row] [32, 34, 34, 36, 36, 38] times, join in first sc. Fasten off. Rep around rem Armhole. *([105, 117, 114, 123, 135, 153] sc)* ●

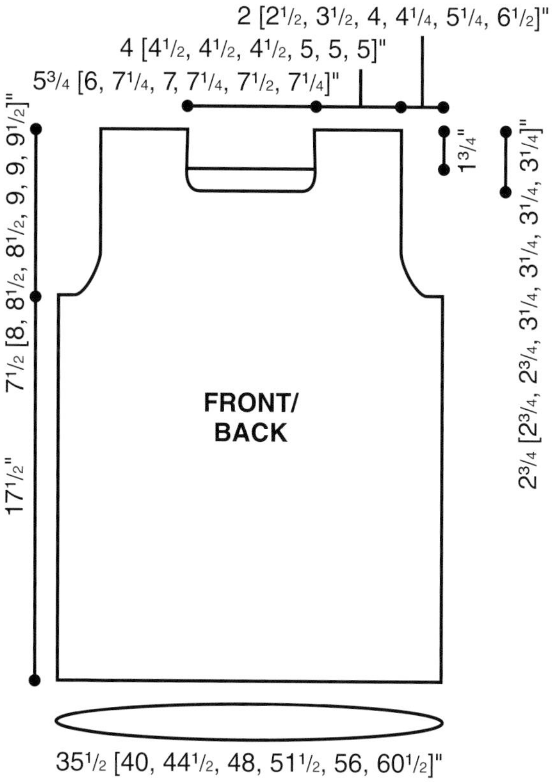
2 [2 1/2, 3 1/2, 4, 4 1/4, 5 1/4, 6 1/2]"
4 [4 1/2, 4 1/2, 4 1/2, 5, 5, 5]"
5 3/4 [6, 7 1/4, 7, 7 1/4, 7 1/2, 7 1/4]"
7 1/2 [8, 8 1/2, 8 1/2, 9, 9, 9 1/2]"
17 1/2"
1 3/4"
2 3/4 [2 3/4, 2 3/4, 3 1/4, 3 1/4, 3 1/4, 3 1/4]"
FRONT/
BACK
35 1/2 [40, 44 1/2, 48, 51 1/2, 56, 60 1/2]"

Breezy Blooms Top

Skill Level

■■■▷ EXPERIENCED

Finished Sizes

Instructions given fit size small; changes for medium, large, X-large, 2X-large, 3X-large and 4X-large are in [ ].

Finished Measurement

Bust: 35½ inches *(small)* [40 inches *(medium)*, 44½ inches *(large)*, 48 inches *(X-large)*, 51½ inches *(2X-large)*, 56 inches *(3X-large)*, 60½ inches *(4X-large)*]

Materials

- Omega Dalia size 3 crochet cotton (3½ oz/404 yds/100g per ball):
  2 [2, 3, 3, 4, 4, 5] ball, #518 ecru
  1 ball #583 leaf green
- Size G/6/4mm crochet hook or size needed to obtain gauge
- Tapestry needle

Gauge

Motif = 1¾ inches x 1¾ inches; 2 pattern reps and 7 rows in lace pattern = 4 inches

Pattern Notes

Weave in loose ends as work progresses.

Join with slip stitch as indicated unless otherwise stated.

Motifs are joined in a continuous round, but are broken down into rows for clarification *(see General Motif Assembly Diagram on page 43)*.

Chain-3 at beginning of row counts as first double crochet unless otherwise stated.

Half double crochet in first single crochet at end of round counts as last chain-3 space.

Chain-2, double crochet in first single crochet at end of round counts as last chain-3 space.

Chain-4 at beginning of round counts as chain-1 and double crochet unless otherwise stated.

Special Stitches

Picot: Ch 3, sl st in st indicated.

Cluster (cl): Holding back last lp of each dc on hook, 3 dc in indicated sp, yo and draw through all 4 lps on hook.

Top

Yoke

Motif

Make 53 [60, 59, 66, 75, 77, 79].

Rnd 1 (RS): With green, ch 4, (2 dc, [ch 2, 3 dc] 3 times) in 4th ch from hook *(beg 3 sk chs count as a dc)*, ch 2, **join** *(see Pattern Notes)* in 3rd ch of beg 3 sk chs. Fasten off. *(12 dc)*

Joining Motifs

Row 1 (RS): Join ecru in any ch-2 sp of first **Motif** *(see Pattern Notes)*, **ch 3** *(see Pattern Notes)*, 2 dc in same sp, [ch 1, (3 dc, ch 3, 3 dc) in next ch-2 sp] twice, [*ch 1, 3 dc in next ch-2 sp, ch 3, 3 dc in ch-2 sp of new Motif, sl st in next ch-1 sp of previous Motif, 3 dc in next ch-2 sp of working Motif, ch 1, sl st in next ch-2 sp of previous Motif*, ch 1, 3 dc in same ch-2 sp of working Motif, ch 1, (3 dc, ch 3, 3 dc) in next ch-2 sp] 16 [18, 20, 22, 24, 26, 28] times, rep from * to *, leave rem sts of last Motif unworked. *(312 [348, 384, 420, 456, 492, 528] dc)*

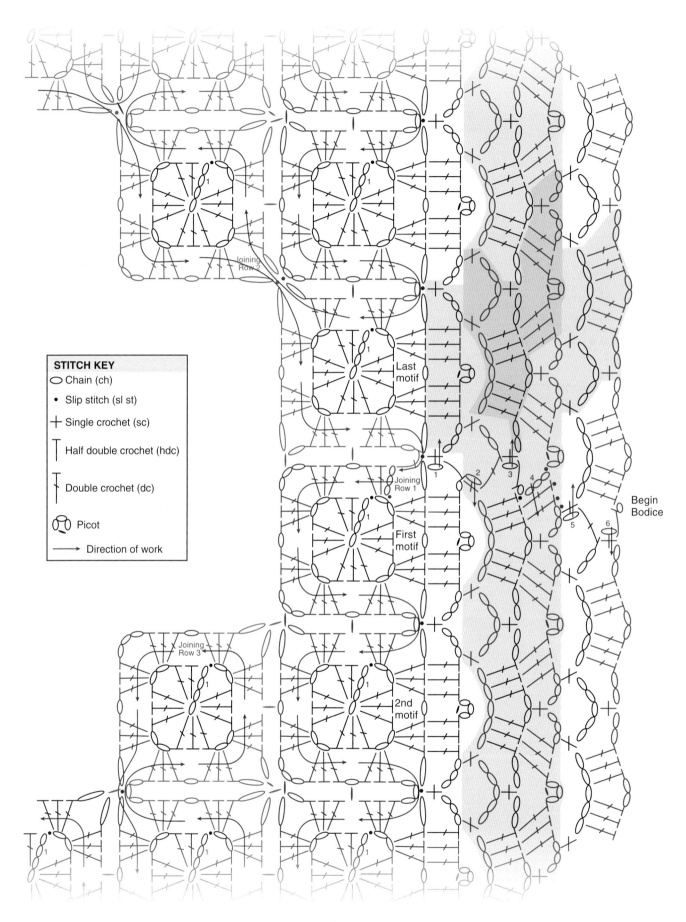

STITCH KEY
⬭ Chain (ch)
• Slip stitch (sl st)
╪ Single crochet (sc)
┬ Half double crochet (hdc)
┼ Double crochet (dc)
🔘 Picot
→ Direction of work

Breezy Blooms Top
Motif Joining Stitch Diagram
Note: *Reps shown in gray.*

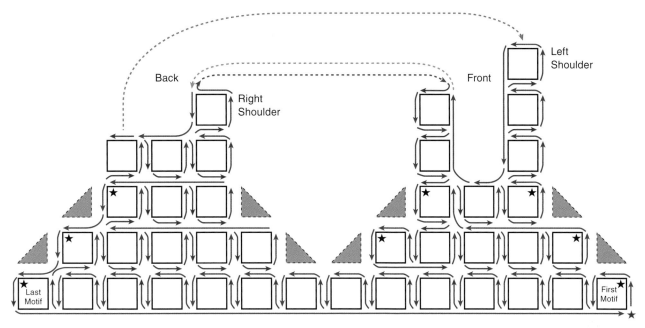

Breezy Blooms Top
General Motif Assembly Diagram

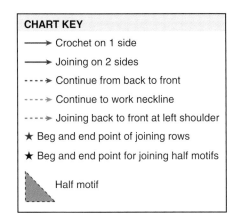

CHART KEY

⟶ Crochet on 1 side

⟶ Joining on 2 sides

----▸ Continue from back to front

----▸ Continue to work neckline

----▸ Joining back to front at left shoulder

★ Beg and end point of joining rows

★ Beg and end point for joining half motifs

◤ Half motif

Row 2: Working in opposite direction *(see General Motif Assembly Diagram)*, ch 1, 3 dc in ch-2 sp of new Motif, sl st in next ch-1 sp of next-to-last Motif, [*3 dc in next ch-2 sp of working Motif, ch 1, sl st in next sl st of row below, ch 1, 3 dc in same sp of working Motif*, 3 dc in next ch-2 sp, ch 3, 3 dc in ch-2 sp of new Motif, sl st in next ch-1 sp of previous Motif, 3 dc in next ch-2 sp of working Motif, ch 1, sl st in same sl st of row below, ch 1, 3 dc in same sp of working Motif, sl st in next ch-1 sp of row below]
6 [7, 6, 7, 8, 8, 8] times, rep from * to *. *(117 [135, 117, 135, 153, 153, 153] dc)*

Note: *For desired size, follow Assembly Diagram on pages 48–50 when working following rows.*

Row 3: Working in opposite direction, ch 1, (3 dc, ch 3, 3 dc) in next ch-2 sp, *ch 1, 3 dc in next ch-3 sp, ch 1, sl st in next ch-3 sp**, ch 1, 3 dc in next ch-3 sp, rep from * across to next-to-last Motif, ending last rep at **, leave rem sts of last Motif unworked. *(39 [45, 39, 45, 51, 51, 51] dc)*

Row 4: Working in opposite direction, ch 1, 3 dc in ch-2 sp of new Motif, sl st in next ch-1 sp of next-to-last Motif, *3 dc in next ch-2 sp of working Motif, sl st in next sl st of row below, ch 1, 3 dc in same sp of working Motif**, ch 1, 3 dc in next ch-2 sp, ch 3, 3 dc in ch-2 sp of new Motif, sl st in next ch-1 sp of previous Motif, 3 dc in next ch-2 sp of working Motif, ch 1, sl st in same sl st of row below, ch 1, 3 dc in same sp of working Motif, sl st in next ch-1 sp of row below, rep from * across to next-to-last Motif, ending last rep at **, leave rem sts of last Motif unworked. *(81 [99, 81, 99, 117, 117, 117] dc)*

Row 5: Working in opposite direction, ch 1, (3 dc, ch 3, 3 dc) in next ch-2 sp, *ch 1, 3 dc in next ch-2 sp, ch 1, sl st in next ch-3 sp**, ch 1, 3 dc in next ch-2 sp, rep from * across, ending last rep at **. *(33 [39, 33, 39, 45, 45, 45] dc)*

Row 6: Working in opposite direction, ch 1, 3 dc in ch-2 sp of new Motif, *sl st in next ch-1 sp of row below, 3 dc in next ch-3 sp of working Motif, ch 1, sl st in next sl st of row below, ch 1, 3 dc in same sp of working Motif**, ch 1, 3 dc in next ch-2 sp, ch 3, 3 dc in ch-2 sp of new Motif, sl st in next ch-1 sp of previous Motif, 3 dc in next ch-3 sp of working Motif, ch 1, sl st in same sl st of row below, ch 1, 3 dc in same sp of working Motif, rep from * across, ending last rep at **. *(81 [99, 81, 99, 117, 117, 117] dc)*

Right Shoulder

Row 1: *Ch 1, (3 dc, ch 3, 3 dc) in next ch-2 sp, ch 1, 3 dc in next ch-3 sp*, ch 1, sl st in next ch-3 sp, ch 1, **3 dc in ch-3 sp of new Motif, sl st in next ch-1 sp of previous Motif, 3 dc in next ch-3 sp of working Motif, ch 1, sl st in next ch-3 sp of previous Motif, ch 1, 3 dc in same sp of working Motif**, [ch 1, (3 dc, ch 3, 3 dc) in next ch-2 sp, ch 1, 3 dc in next ch-3 sp, ch 3, 3 dc in ch-3 sp of new Motif, sl st in next ch-1 sp of previous Motif, 3 dc in next ch-3 sp of working Motif, ch 1, sl st in next ch-3 sp of previous Motif, ch 1, 3 dc in same sp of working Motif] 4 [4, 5, 5, 6, 6, 6] times. *(90 [90, 108, 108, 126, 126, 126] dc)*

Front

Row 1: Work this row as follows:

A. Ch 1, 3 dc in next ch-2 sp, ch 3, *3 dc in ch-2 sp of new Motif, sl st in next ch-1 sp of previous Motif, 3 dc in next ch-2 sp of working Motif*;

B. ch 1, sl st in next sl st, **ch 1, 3 dc in same ch-2 sp of working Motif, ch 1**, (3 dc, ch 3, 3 dc) in next ch-2 sp, ch 1, 3 dc in next ch-2 sp, ch 1, sk 2 [2, 4, 4, 4, 5, 6] Motifs from Back, sl st in next sl st of row below, ch 1, 3 dc in same ch-2 sp of working Motif, sl st in next ch-1 sp of row below;

C. 3 dc in next ch-2 sp of working Motif, ch 1, sl st in next sl st of row below, ch 1, 3 dc in next ch-2 sp of next Motif, sl st in next ch-1 sp of row below;

D. 3 dc in next ch-2 sp of working Motif, ch 1, sl st in next sl st of row below, rep from ** to **, dc in next ch-2 sp of working Motif, ch 1, sl st in next ch-3 sp *(in row above)*, ch 1;

E. rep from * to *, [ch 1, sl st in next sl st, ch 1, 3 dc in same ch-2 sp of working Motif, sl st in next ch-1 sp of row below, 3 dc in next ch-2 sp of working Motif, ch 1, sl st in next sl st of row below;

F. 3 dc in next ch-3 sp, ch 3, 3 dc in ch-2 sp of new Motif, sl st in next ch-1 sp of previous Motif, 3 dc in next ch-2 sp of working Motif] 4 [5, 4, 5, 6, 6, 6] times, ch 1, sl st in next sl st, ch 1, 3 dc in same ch-2 sp of working Motif, st in next ch-1 sp of row below, 3 dc in next ch-2 sp of working Motif, ch 1, sl st in next sl st of row below. *(126 [144, 126, 144, 162, 162, 162] dc)*

Row 2: (3 dc, ch 3, 3 dc) in next ch-2 sp, [*ch 1, 3 dc in next ch-2 sp, ch 1*, sl st in next ch-3 sp, ch 1, 3 dc in next ch-3 sp] 4 [5, 4, 5, 6, 6, 6] times, ch 1, 3 dc in next ch-2 sp, ch 1, sl st in next sl st. *(33 [39, 33, 39, 45, 45, 45] dc)*

Row 3: Ch 1, 3 dc in next ch-2 sp *(in row above)*, ch 1, 3 dc in next ch-2 sp, ch 1, sl st in next ch-3 *(in row above)*, ch 1, *3 dc in ch-3 sp of new Motif, sl st in ch-1 sp of previous Motif, 3 dc in next ch-2 of working Motif, ch 1, sl st in next sl st, ch 1, 3 dc in same ch-2 sp of working Motif, sl st in next ch-1 sp of row below, 3 dc in next ch-2 of working Motif, ch 1, sl st in next sl st of row below, ch 1, 3 dc in same ch-2 sp of working Motif**, ch 1, 3 dc in next ch-3 sp, ch 3, rep from * across to next-to-last Motif, ending last rep at **, leave rem sts of last Motif unworked. *(75 [93, 75, 93, 111, 111, 111] dc)*

Left Shoulder

Ch 1, (3 dc, ch 3, 3 dc) in next ch-2 sp, ch 1, 3 dc in next ch-3 sp, ch 1, sl st in next ch-3 sp, **ch 1, 3 dc in ch-3 sp of new Motif, sl st in ch-1 sp of previous Motif, 3 dc in next ch-2 sp of working Motif, ch 1, sl st in next ch-3 sp of previous Motif, ch 1, 3 dc in same ch-3 sp of working Motif**, [rep from * to *, ch 3, rep from ** to **] 2 [2, 3, 3, 4, 4, 4] times, [ch 1, (3 dc, ch 3, 3 dc) in next ch-2 sp] 2 times. *(66 [66, 84, 84, 102, 102, 102] dc)*

Neckline

[Ch 1, 3 dc in next ch-2 sp, ch 1, sl st in next ch-3 sp, ch 1, 3 dc in ch-2 sp of next Motif] 2 [2, 3, 3, 4, 4, 4] times, ch 1, 3 dc in next ch-2 sp, [ch 1, sl st in next sl st, {ch 1, 3 dc in next ch-2 sp} twice] 3 [4, 3, 4, 5, 5, 5] times, [ch 1, sl st in next ch-3 sp, {ch 1, 3 dc in next ch-2 sp} twice] 3 [3, 4, 4, 5, 5, 5] times, ch 1, sl st in next sl st, ch 1, 3 dc in next ch-2 sp, [ch 1, 3 dc in next ch-2 sp, ch 1, sl st in next ch-3 sp, ch 1, 3 dc in ch-2 sp of next Motif] 2 [2, 3, 3, 4, 4, 4] times, ch 1, 3 dc in next ch-2 sp, sl st in corresponding ch-3 of Left Shoulder, ch 1, 3 dc in next ch-3 sp of next Motif, sl st in next ch-1 sp of left shoulder, 3 dc in next ch-3 sp of working Motif, ch 1, sl st in next ch-3 sp of left shoulder, ch 1, 3 dc in same sp of working Motif. *(78 [90, 90, 102, 126, 126] dc)*

Left Armhole

Ch 1, 3 dc in next ch-3 sp, ch 1, sl st in next ch-3 sp, [rep from * to *] 2 times, ch 1, sl st in next sl st, ch 1, 3 dc in next ch-3 sp, ch 1, (3 dc, ch 3, 3 dc) in next ch-2 sp, ch 1, 3 dc in next ch-3 sp, ch 1, sl st in next sl st, [ch 1, 3 dc in next ch-3 sp] twice, ch 1, sl st in corresponding ch-3 sp of first Motif at other end of row 1, ch 1, 3 dc in same sp of last Motif, sl st in ch-1 sp of first Motif, 3 dc in next ch-3 sp of last Motif, ch 1, join with dc in first dc of first Motif. *(33 dc)*

Bottom Edge

Ch 1, 3 dc in same sp of last Motif, *ch 1, 3 dc in next ch-2 sp, ch 1**, sl st in next ch-3 sp, ch 1, 3 dc in next ch-2 sp, rep from * around, ending last rep at **, ch 1, join with dc in first dc of row 1, turn. Do not Fasten off. *(108 [120, 132, 144, 156, 168, 180] dc)* 24 dc per Motif; *1272 [1440, 1416, 1584, 1800, 1848, 1896] dc)*

Bodice

Rnd 1 (WS): Ch 1, sc in same st, *ch 3, dc in next 3 dc, **picot** *(see Special Stitches)* in dc just made, sk next ch-1 sp, dc in next 3 dc**, ch 3, sk next ch sp, sc in next sl st, rep from * around, ending last rep at **, ch 1, join with hdc in first sc, turn. *(108 [120, 132, 144, 156, 168, 180] dc, 18 [20, 22, 24, 26, 28, 30] picots, 18 [20, 22, 24, 26, 28, 30] sc, 36 [40, 44, 48, 52, 56, 60] ch sps)*

Rnd 2: Ch 1, sc in same sp, *ch 5, sk next 7 sts, sc in next ch-3 sp**, ch 5, sk next sc, sc in next ch-3 sp, rep from * around, ending last rep at **, **ch 2, dc in first sc** *(see Pattern Notes)*, ch 1, turn. *(36 [40, 44, 48, 52, 56, 60] ch-5 sps)*

Rnd 3: Ch 1, sc in dc, *ch 2, sk next sc, (3 dc, ch 2, 3 dc) in next ch-5 sp**, ch 2, sk next sc, sc in next ch-5 sp, rep from * around, ending last rep at **, **hdc in first sc** *(see Pattern Notes)*, turn. *(108 [120, 132, 144, 156, 168, 180] dc, 18 [20, 22, 24, 26, 28, 30] sc)*

Rnd 4: Ch 1, sl st in first dc, ch 3, dc in next 2 dc, *ch 3, sc in next ch-2 sp, ch 3, dc in next 3 dc, picot in dc just made, sk next 5 sts**, dc in next 3 dc, rep from * around, ending last rep at **, join, sl st in next 2 dc and next ch-3 sp, ch 1, turn.

Rnds 5–7: Rep rnds 2–4.

Rnds 8 & 9: Rep rnds 2–3.

Shape A-Line

Rnd 1: Sl st in first dc, ch 3, dc in next 2 dc, *ch 3, (sc, ch 3, sc) in next ch-2 sp, ch 3, dc in next 3 dc, picot in dc just made, sk next 5 sts, dc in next 3 dc, ch 3, sc in next ch-2 sp, ch 3, dc in next 3 dc, picot in dc just made, sk next 5 sts**, dc in next 3 dc, rep from * around, ending last rep at **, join, sl st in next 2 dc and next ch-3 sp, turn. *(108 [120, 132, 144, 156, 168, 180] dc, 18 [20, 22, 24, 26, 28, 30] picots, 27 [30, 33, 36, 39, 42, 45] sc, 55 [50, 55, 60, 65, 70, 75] ch-3 sps)*

Rnd 2: Ch 1, sc in same sp, *ch 5, sk next 7 sts, sc in next ch-3 sp, ch 5, sk next sc, sc in next ch-3 sp, ch 5, sk next 7 sts, (sc, ch 3, sc) in next ch-3 sp, ch 5, sk next 5 sts**, (sc, ch 3, sc) in next ch-3 sp, rep from * around, ending last rep at **, sc in first ch sp, ch 1, hdc in first sc, turn. *(36 [40, 44, 48, 52, 56, 60] ch-5 sps, 18 [20, 22, 24, 26, 28, 30] ch-3 sps)*

Rnd 3: Ch 1, sc in dc, *ch 2, sk next sc, (3 dc, ch 2, 3 dc) in next ch-5 sp**, ch 2, sk next sc, sc in next ch sp, rep from * around, ending last rep at **, hdc in first sc, ch 1, turn. *(162 [180, 198, 216, 234, 252, 270] dc, 27 [30, 33, 36, 39, 42, 45] sc)*

Rnd 4: Sl st in first dc, ch 3, dc in next 2 dc, *ch 3, sc in next ch-2 sp, ch 3, dc in next 3 dc, picot in dc just made, sk next 5 sts**, dc in next 3 dc, rep from * around, ending last rep at **, join, sl st in next 2 dc and next ch-3 sp, turn. *(162 [180, 198, 216, 234, 252, 270] dc, 27 [30, 33, 36, 39, 42, 45] picots, 27 [30, 33, 36, 39, 42, 45] sc, 54 [60, 66, 72, 78, 84, 90] ch sps)*

Rnd 5: Ch 1, sc in same sp, *ch 5, sk next 7 sts, sc in next ch-3 sp**, ch 5, sk next sc, sc in next ch-3 sp, rep from * around, ending last rep at **, ch 2, dc in first sc, ch 1, turn. *(54 [60, 66, 72, 78, 84, 90] ch-5 sps)*

Rnds 6–20 [6–20, 6–17, 6–17, 6–17, 6–17, 6–17]: [Rep rnds 3–5] 5 [5, 4, 4, 4, 4, 4] times.

Rnds 21 & 22 [21 & 22, 18 & 19, 18 & 19, 18 & 19, 18 & 19, 18 & 19]: Rep rnds 3 and 4. Fasten off.

Half Motif
Make 8.

First Half Motif
Row 1: Ch 4 *(see Pattern Notes)* sl st in ch-3 sp *(see Half Motif Stitch Diagram)*, ch 1, 2 dc in 4th ch from hook, ch 1, sl st in next ch-1 sp on completed Motif, ch 1, 3 dc in same ch as last 2 dc made, ch 1, sl st in next sl st on completed Motif, ch 1, 3 dc in same ch as last dc made, ch 1, sl st in next ch-1 sp on completed Motif, ch 1, 3 dc in same ch as last dc made, ch 1, sl st in next ch-3 sp on completed Motif. Fasten off. *(12 dc)*

Neck Edging
With RS of Back Neck Edge facing, sk 1 ch sp from Right Shoulder, join ecru in next dc, ch 1, *[sc in next dc, sk next dc, (sc, ch 3, sc) in next ch-1 sp, sk next dc, sc in next dc, sc in next ch-3 sp, (sc, ch 3, sc) in next sl st, sc in next ch-3 sp, sk next dc] 2 [3, 2, 3, 4, 3, 4] times, sc in next dc, sk next dc, (sc, ch 3, sc) in next ch-1 sp, sk next dc, sc in next dc, sk next dc, **cl** *(see Special Stitches)* in next ch-3 sp, picot in st just made, sk next sl st, cl in next ch-3 sp, sk next dc, [sc in next dc, sk next dc, (sc, ch 3, sc) in next ch-1 sp, sk next dc, sc in next dc, sc in next ch-3 sp, (sc, ch 3, sc) in next sl st, sc in next ch-3 sp, sk next dc] 2 [2, 3, 3, 4, 4, 4] times, sc in next dc, sk next dc, (sc, ch 3, sc) in next ch-1 sp, sk next dc, sc in next dc, sk next dc, cl in next ch-3 sp, picot in st just made, sk next sl st, cl in next ch-3 sp, sk next dc, rep from * around, join in first sc. Fasten off. *(80 [96, 96, 112, 144, 128, 144] sc, 20 [24, 24, 28, 36, 32, 36] ch-3 sps, 4 picots)*

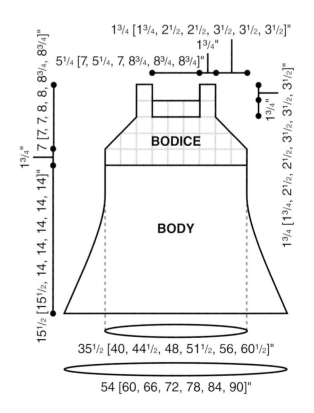

1³/₄ [1³/₄, 2¹/₂, 2¹/₂, 3¹/₂, 3¹/₂, 3¹/₂]"

1³/₄"

5¹/₄ [7, 5¹/₄, 7, 8³/₄, 8³/₄, 8³/₄]"

1³/₄"

1³/₄ [1³/₄, 2¹/₂, 2¹/₂, 3¹/₂, 3¹/₂, 3¹/₂]"

7 [7, 7, 8, 8, 8³/₄, 8³/₄]"

1³/₄"

15¹/₂ [15¹/₂, 14, 14, 14, 14, 14]"

BODICE

BODY

35¹/₂ [40, 44¹/₂, 48, 51¹/₂, 56, 60¹/₂]"

54 [60, 66, 72, 78, 84, 90]"

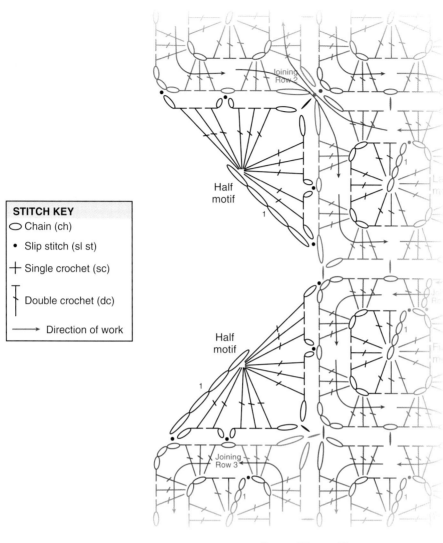

STITCH KEY
- ◯ Chain (ch)
- • Slip stitch (sl st)
- + Single crochet (sc)
- ⊤ Double crochet (dc)
- → Direction of work

Half motif

Half motif

Joining Row 3

Breezy Blooms Top
Half Motif Stitch Diagram

Armhole Edging

Sizes Small & Medium Only

With RS facing, join ecru at center of 1 underarm, ch 1, (sc, ch 3, sc) in same st, *[sc in next ch-1 sp, sc in next row, (sc, ch 3, sc) in next ch, sc in next row, sc in next ch-1 sp, (sc, ch 3, sc) in next sl st]* 2 times, [sc in next ch-3 sp, sk next dc, sc in next dc, sk next dc, (sc, ch 3, sc) in next ch-1 sp, sk next dc, sc in next dc, sk next dc**, sc in next ch-3 sp, (sc, ch 3, sc) in next sl st] 4 times, rep from * to *,sc in next ch-1 sp, sc in next row, (sc, ch 3, sc) in next ch, sc in next row, sc in next ch-1 sp, join in first sc. Fasten off.

Rep for 2nd Armhole.

Sizes Large, X-Large, 2X-Large, 3X-Large & 4X-Large Only

With RS facing, join ecru at right end of 1 underarm, ch 1, (sc, ch 3, sc) in same st, [sc in next ch-3 sp, sk next dc, sc in next dc, sk next dc, (sc, ch 3, sc) in next ch-1 sp, sk next dc, sc in next dc, sk next dc, sc in next ch-3 sp, (sc, ch 3, sc) in next sl st] 0 [0, 1, 2, 2] time(s), [sc in next ch-1 sp, sc in next row, (sc, ch 3, sc) in next ch, sc in next row, sc in next ch-1 sp, (sc, ch 3, sc) in next sl st] twice, [sc in next ch-3 sp, sk next dc, sc in next dc, sk next dc, (sc, ch 3, sc) in next ch-1 sp, sk next dc, sc in next dc, sk next dc, sc in next ch-3 sp, (sc, ch 3, sc) in next sl st] 5 [5, 6, 6, 6] times, sc in next ch-1 sp, sc in next row, (sc, ch 3, sc) in next ch, sc in next row, sc in next ch-1 sp, (sc, ch 3, sc) in next sl st, sc in next ch-1 sp, sc in next row, (sc, ch 3, sc) in next

ch, sc in next row, sc in next ch-1 sp, join in first sc. Fasten off.

Rep for 2nd Armhole. ●

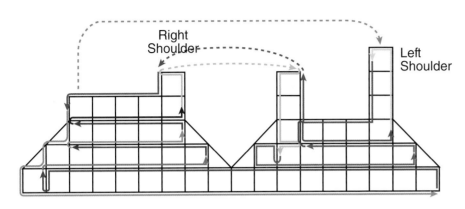

Breezy Blooms Top
Size S Assembly Diagram

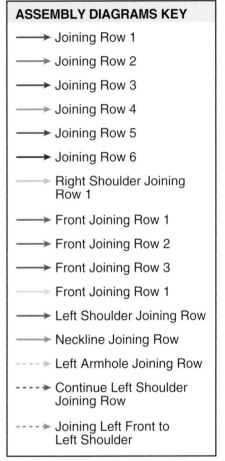

ASSEMBLY DIAGRAMS KEY
→ Joining Row 1
→ Joining Row 2
→ Joining Row 3
→ Joining Row 4
→ Joining Row 5
→ Joining Row 6
→ Right Shoulder Joining Row 1
→ Front Joining Row 1
→ Front Joining Row 2
→ Front Joining Row 3
→ Front Joining Row 1
→ Left Shoulder Joining Row
→ Neckline Joining Row
---→ Left Armhole Joining Row
---→ Continue Left Shoulder Joining Row
---→ Joining Left Front to Left Shoulder

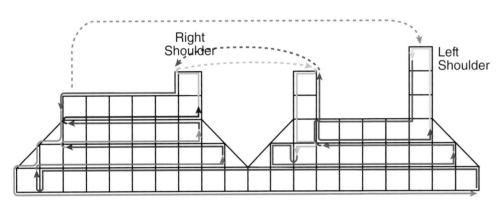

Breezy Blooms Top
Size M Assembly Diagram

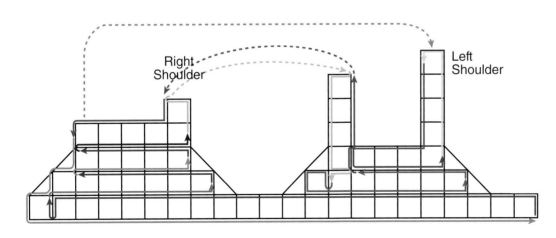

Breezy Blooms Top
Size L Assembly Diagram

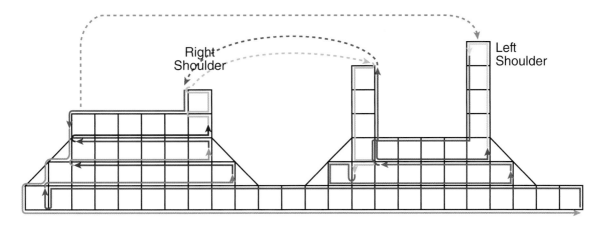

Breezy Blooms Top
Size XL Assembly Diagram

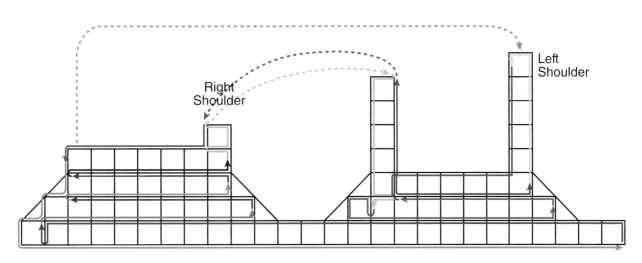

Breezy Blooms Top
Size 2XL Assembly Diagram

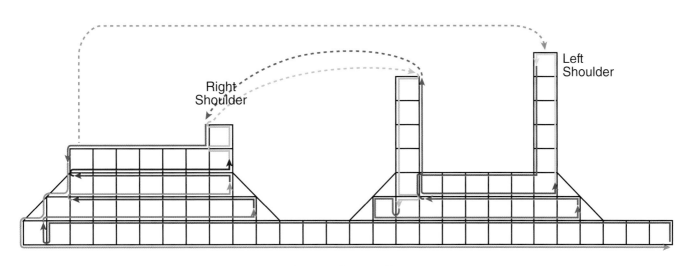

Breezy Blooms Top
Size 3XL Assembly Diagram

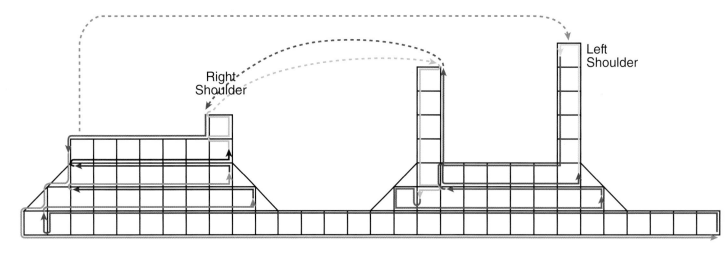

Breezy Blooms Top
Size 4XL Assembly Diagram

ASSEMBLY DIAGRAMS KEY
→ Joining Row 1
→ Joining Row 2
→ Joining Row 3
→ Joining Row 4
→ Joining Row 5
→ Joining Row 6
→ Right Shoulder Joining Row 1
→ Front Joining Row 1
→ Front Joining Row 2
→ Front Joining Row 3
→ Front Joining Row 1
→ Left Shoulder Joining Row
→ Neckline Joining Row
---→ Left Armhole Joining Row
---→ Continue Left Shoulder Joining Row
---→ Joining Left Front to Left Shoulder

STITCH GUIDE

STITCH ABBREVIATIONS

beg	begin/begins/beginning
bpdc	back post double crochet
bpsc	back post single crochet
bptr	back post treble crochet
CC	contrasting color
ch(s)	chain(s)
ch-	refers to chain or space previously made (i.e., ch-1 space)
ch sp(s)	chain space(s)
cl(s)	cluster(s)
cm	centimeter(s)
dc	double crochet (singular/plural)
dc dec	double crochet 2 or more stitches together, as indicated
dec	decrease/decreases/decreasing
dtr	double treble crochet
ext	extended
fpdc	front post double crochet
fpsc	front post single crochet
fptr	front post treble crochet
g	gram(s)
hdc	half double crochet
hdc dec	half double crochet 2 or more stitches together, as indicated
inc	increase/increases/increasing
lp(s)	loop(s)
MC	main color
mm	millimeter(s)
oz	ounce(s)
pc	popcorn(s)
rem	remain/remains/remaining
rep(s)	repeat(s)
rnd(s)	round(s)
RS	right side
sc	single crochet (singular/plural)
sc dec	single crochet 2 or more stitches together, as indicated
sk	skip/skipped/skipping
sl st(s)	slip stitch(es)
sp(s)	space(s)/spaced
st(s)	stitch(es)
tog	together
tr	treble crochet
trtr	triple treble
WS	wrong side
yd(s)	yard(s)
yo	yarn over

YARN CONVERSION

OUNCES TO GRAMS		GRAMS TO OUNCES	
1	28.4	25	⅞
2	56.7	40	1⅔
3	85.0	50	1¾
4	113.4	100	3½

UNITED STATES		UNITED KINGDOM
sl st (slip stitch)	=	sc (single crochet)
sc (single crochet)	=	dc (double crochet)
hdc (half double crochet)	=	htr (half treble crochet)
dc (double crochet)	=	tr (treble crochet)
tr (treble crochet)	=	dtr (double treble crochet)
dtr (double treble crochet)	=	ttr (triple treble crochet)
skip	=	miss

Single crochet decrease (sc dec): (Insert hook, yo, draw lp through) in each of the sts indicated, yo, draw through all lps on hook.

Example of 2-sc dec

Half double crochet decrease (hdc dec): (Yo, insert hook, yo, draw lp through) in each of the sts indicated, yo, draw through all lps on hook.

Example of 2-hdc dec

Reverse single crochet (reverse sc):
Ch 1, sk first st, working from left to right, insert hook in next st from front to back, draw up lp on hook, yo and draw through both lps on hook.

Chain (ch): Yo, pull through lp on hook.

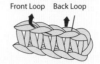

Single crochet (sc): Insert hook in st, yo, pull through st, yo, pull through both lps on hook.

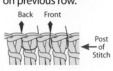

Double crochet (dc): Yo, insert hook in st, yo, pull through st, [yo, pull through 2 lps] twice.

Double crochet decrease (dc dec): (Yo, insert hook, yo, draw lp through, yo, draw through 2 lps on hook) in each of the sts indicated, yo, draw through all lps on hook.

Example of 2-dc dec

Front loop (front lp) Back loop (back lp)

Front Loop   Back Loop

Front post stitch (fp): Back post stitch (bp): When working post st, insert hook from right to left around post of st on previous row.

Back   Front

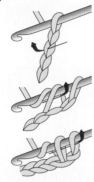

Post of Stitch

Half double crochet (hdc): Yo, insert hook in st, yo, pull through st, yo, pull through all 3 lps on hook.

Double treble crochet (dtr): Yo 3 times, insert hook in st, yo, pull through st, [yo, pull through 2 lps] 4 times.

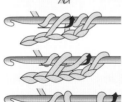

Treble crochet decrease (tr dec): Holding back last lp of each st, tr in each of the sts indicated, yo, pull through all lps on hook.

Example of 2-tr dec

Slip stitch (sl st): Insert hook in st, pull through both lps on hook.

Chain color change (ch color change) Yo with new color, draw through last lp on hook.

Double crochet color change (dc color change) Drop first color, yo with new color, draw through last 2 lps of st.

Treble crochet (tr): Yo twice, insert hook in st, yo, pull through st, [yo, pull through 2 lps] 3 times.

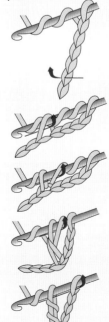

Metric Conversion Charts

METRIC CONVERSIONS

yards	x	.9144	=	metres (m)
yards	x	91.44	=	centimetres (cm)
inches	x	2.54	=	centimetres (cm)
inches	x	25.40	=	millimetres (mm)
inches	x	.0254	=	metres (m)

centimetres	x	.3937	=	inches
metres	x	1.0936	=	yards

INCHES INTO MILLIMETRES & CENTIMETRES (Rounded off slightly)

inches	mm	cm	inches	cm	inches	cm	inches	cm
1/8	3	0.3	5	12.5	21	53.5	38	96.5
1/4	6	0.6	5 1/2	14	22	56	39	99
3/8	10	1	6	15	23	58.5	40	101.5
1/2	13	1.3	7	18	24	61	41	104
5/8	15	1.5	8	20.5	25	63.5	42	106.5
3/4	20	2	9	23	26	66	43	109
7/8	22	2.2	10	25.5	27	68.5	44	112
1	25	2.5	11	28	28	71	45	114.5
1 1/4	32	3.2	12	30.5	29	73.5	46	117
1 1/2	38	3.8	13	33	30	76	47	119.5
1 3/4	45	4.5	14	35.5	31	79	48	122
2	50	5	15	38	32	81.5	49	124.5
2 1/2	65	6.5	16	40.5	33	84	50	127
3	75	7.5	17	43	34	86.5		
3 1/2	90	9	18	46	35	89		
4	100	10	19	48.5	36	91.5		
4 1/2	115	11.5	20	51	37	94		

KNITTING NEEDLES CONVERSION CHART

Canada/U.S.	0	1	2	3	4	5	6	7	8	9	10	10½	11	13	15
Metric (mm)	2	2¼	2¾	3¼	3½	3¾	4	4½	5	5½	6	6½	8	9	10

CROCHET HOOKS CONVERSION CHART

Canada/U.S.	1/B	2/C	3/D	4/E	5/F	6/G	8/H	9/I	10/J	10½/K	N
Metric (mm)	2.25	2.75	3.25	3.5	3.75	4.25	5	5.5	6	6.5	9.0

 Summer Tops is published by Annie's, 306 East Parr Road, Berne, IN 46711. Printed in USA. Copyright © 2015 Annie's. All rights reserved. This publication may not be reproduced in part or in whole without written permission from the publisher.

RETAIL STORES: If you would like to carry this publication or any other Annie's publication, visit AnniesWSL.com.

Every effort has been made to ensure that the instructions in this publication are complete and accurate. We cannot, however, take responsibility for human error, typographical mistakes or variations in individual work. Please visit AnniesCustomerService.com to check for pattern updates.

ISBN: 978-1-57367-700-4

1 2 3 4 5 6 7 8 9